ON WHAT THERE MUST BE

On What There Must Be

• by •

Ross Harrison

CLARENDON PRESS
OXFORD
1974

Oxford University Press, Ely House, London, W. 1

GLASGOW NEW YORK TORONTO MELBOURNE WELLINGTON
CAPE TOWN IBADAN NAIROBI DAR ES SALAAM LUSAKA ADDIS ABABA
DELHI BOMBAY CALCUTTA MADRAS KARACHI LAHORE DACCA
KUALA LUMPUR SINGAPORE HONG KONG TOKYO

ISBN 0 19 824507 6

© OXFORD UNIVERSITY PRESS 1974

*Printed in Great Britain
by Butler & Tanner Ltd
Frome and London*

To
Gillian

PREFACE

THE title of this book is a half quotation of the title of Quine's famous article 'On What There Is' (which Quine, in turn, borrowed from Russell). This is not without specific point, since the thesis of the present work is that there are certain features which are essential in any world which we are able to understand and that, therefore, some at least of our ontological commitments (to use Quine's phrase) are not a matter of choice or convention.

The book is an inquiry into the basic conditions which must be met by any comprehensible world. In particular, I consider the importance of space and time, of existence unperceived, of publicity and action, and of natural laws. These are examined in a single argument which extends from Chapter Three to Chapter Seven and in the course of which the essential features of any comprehensible world are either assumed or derived. In Chapter Two, before this argument begins, I introduce and argue for the methods by which this general argument is developed.

In Chapter One I attempt to show why it is important to consider the essential features of any comprehensible world. This chapter forms a prolegomenon to the inquiry. The argument in it is of a somewhat more impressionistic nature than the argument later in the inquiry; and so it is probably important to point out that the conclusions reached in the inquiry itself are practically independent of the argument of the first chapter. Those that are totally unconvinced by it may still be persuaded by the general argument which follows.

The work in this book depends upon that of many other people. I should like to single out among them for particular thanks Professors Strawson, Bennett, and Bernard Williams. Apart from the use I have made of their written work, I have also had the benefit of their criticism of parts of what is written here. Those that frown at what remains may easily imagine the kind of horrors that have been removed in response to their patient criticism.

Bristol
4 April 1973

CONTENTS

NOTE ON TRANSLATIONS

QUOTATION from Kant's *Critique of Pure Reason* is from the translation by Norman Kemp Smith (Macmillan, 2nd ed. 1933); from the Leibniz–Clarke correspondence is from Clarke's own translation (ed. H. G. Alexander, Manchester University Press, 1956); and from Wittgenstein is from the translation by G. E. M. Anscombe (Blackwell, 2nd ed., 1958).

CHAPTER ONE

Prolegomenon: The Philosopher's World

§1 PHILOSOPHY is often dismissed by non-philosophers as being merely a misguided competitor to science. This is because it seems both to share the scientific aim of attempting to understand the nature of the world yet also to use inappropriate methods for making such an attempt. Unlike scientists, philosophers neither go into laboratories nor seem to be particularly well informed about what is known by those who do. Instead they feel themselves able to dispense with the services of observation and experiment and so able to work with pure reason alone. Yet a common assumption of both philosophers and non-philosophers is that someone operating with pure reason alone cannot discover the nature of the actual world. Armchair science is not a respectable activity; and it is not clear to the non-philosopher, nor sometimes to the philosopher himself, how philosophy differs from armchair science.

This doubt about whether philosophers may even claim to understand the world, let alone to change it, can be supported by an historical observation. In the seventeenth and eighteenth centuries people who attempted to discover the nature of the world were all called philosophers, irrespective of whether they operated in a manner similar to that of present-day philosophers or in a manner similar to that of present-day scientists. However, those who worked with reference to observation and experiment, and later came to be called scientists, went from discovery to discovery, founded successful technologies, and had obviously seized on an effective method of discovering the nature of the world. Whereas those who operated with the pure exercise of thought alone, although they succeeded in preserving the honorific title of philosophers, did not accumulate discoveries nor start technologies, and so did not seem to have found an effective method of discovering the nature of the world. This is why non-philosophers in general, and scientists in particular, are liable to feel that present-day philosophers operate with an inappropriate method which is at best irrelevant and at worst can lead to dangerous interference with science itself.

The fact that philosophy works independently of observation and experiment, together with the common assumption that nothing about the nature of the world can be discovered by the exercise of pure reason alone, also worries philosophers themselves, and leads them to develop various methods of defending the status of their subject. It would be natural for them to do this by contesting the assumption that the nature of the world cannot be discovered by the pure exercise of thought alone and showing that philosophy has its own independent method of discovering the nature of the world. Yet this is not normally what they do. Instead they hold that philosophy not only has its own methods but also its own subject matter, and that it does not attempt to discover the nature of the world at all. Philosophers, it is held, do not attempt to describe the world but engage in an activity called conceptual analysis; this is a meta-subject and so must not be confused with its base subjects, which are the scientific or other common descriptions given of the world by non-philosophers. This form of defence of philosophy is to be found most clearly expressed by the Logical Positivists, but it is also the one normally used by philosophers working in the present British analytic tradition who would not count themselves as positivists. The Logical Positivists were extremely keen to prevent improper interference in science by philosophy and held strongly that the nature of the world could not be discovered by the pure exercise of thought alone. Yet even they did not think that philosophy would wither away after their anti-metaphysical revolution. They thought, rather, that it had its own proper and separate subject matter in the study of the meaningfulness of scientific language. Philosophy, in Schlick's phrase, is the 'pursuit of meaning', and so will not come into conflict with science, which is the 'pursuit of truth'. The spirit of this defence and demarcation of philosophy by Schlick is repeated by many philosophers in the present analytic tradition.

Such a defence of philosophy presupposes that the notion of a concept or meaning is much clearer than it in fact is. For it is not obvious that concepts can be considered indepen-

dently of observation both of the world and of people's use
of language; and even if they can, it is not obvious that
concepts are sufficiently precise or hard-edged to render
extended study of them profitable. Quite apart from these
possible sources of difficulty, this defence of philosophy has
the extraordinary consequence that those thinkers who are
generally considered to be the greatest philosophers were not
really philosophers at all. For it is quite certain that one
thing which all the historically important philosophers
attempted to do was to describe the nature of the world; and
it also seems clear that they attempted to do this by the use
of reason rather than by reliance on any esoteric fact or theory
available from the science of their day. A rapid recital of some
of the conclusions of these great philosophers makes the
former point quite obvious; while the latter is supported by
the fact that these conclusions are argued about by present-
day philosophers and not just described in histories of science.
The Descartes of the *Meditations*, for example, is unquestion-
ably a philosopher rather than a scientist, and a philosopher
continually discussed by philosophers today. Yet the *Meditations* are expressly concerned with showing that certain things
(the self, God, material things) exist, and with demonstrating
their nature. Similarly, Berkeley was talking about the world
when he said that our food and our clothes, being the immediate objects of our senses, were only ideas or composed of
ideas. It was our present, actual world that Kant was describing
when he concluded that it must consist of objects, the changes
of which were causally connected together. Spinoza and Leibniz
may have produced some strange descriptions, but again it was
the actual world that they took themselves to be describing.

It is certain, therefore, that many of the greatest philosophers attempted to describe the actual world, and that they
attempted to do this by the pure exercise of thought alone
independently of particular observations. Those positivists
and post-positivists, therefore, who defend philosophy by saying that it does not intend to describe the actual world must
also hold that all these great philosophers were radically mistaken in what they were attempting to do, and were indeed
not really philosophers at all. Since this would be too extraordinary a conclusion to accept without adequate explanation, a positivist or post-positivist must at the very least

explain how so many eminent men could have come to make such a mistake.

The most natural way in which a post-positivist philosopher might attempt to show that all these great philosophers were mistaken would be by showing that they were all captivated by one particular erroneous, but persistently beguiling, idea. This is the idea that, if suitably dextrous manipulations are performed with concepts or essences, then conclusions about actual individuals or existents can be obtained. The most famous example of such a procedure is the ontological argument for the existence of God, in which it is supposed that from sheer contemplation of the concept of a god (or of the concept of a good god) it can be derived by reason alone that God must exist. It is usually felt that there is an error in all arguments of this form and that this has been conclusively demonstrated by Kant. Since, according to a positivist, a philosopher working with pure reason alone can only have direct access to concepts, and since these great philosophers nevertheless attempt to arrive at conclusions about existents (about the nature of the actual world), a positivist will naturally hold that they are guilty of a similar error to that embodied in the ontological argument.

Although, however, such an explanation might be applied to Spinoza, and perhaps also Leibniz, with some success, it would not do justice to the other conclusions of the great philosophers mentioned above. In Descartes's *cogito* argument, for example, even though it has an explicitly existential conclusion, this is not a conclusion which follows simply from sheer contemplation of the concept of a self or from contemplation of the concept of myself. So also for Berkeley and Kant; it does not follow merely from contemplation of the concept or an idea that the immediate objects of perception do not exist without the mind, nor do Kant's arguments follow merely from the definition of 'cause' or from contemplation of the concept of an empirically real object. Although these arguments have existential conclusions, these conclusions do not follow merely from the definition of certain terms or from contemplation of the nature of certain concepts. This means that these arguments and conclusions can not be explained away as embodying a similar error to that involved in the ontological argument for the existence of God.

Since these positivist principles lead to the extraordinary conclusion that all these great philosophers were simply mistaken in their aims, and since it does not seem simple to explain such a mistake away, it is important to see whether philosophy might not be better defended by disagreeing with the positivist assumption and allowing that philosophers are able to describe the actual world and that they can do this by pure reason alone, independently of observation or experiment. If, that is, it is held that the great philosophers were not simply mistaken, then the question must arise of whether, after all, they might not have been justified in attempting to describe the world while exercising pure reason alone; and, if they were, how they could do it.

This question, which might be called in Kantian terms the question of how pure philosophy is possible, is the question which will be studied in this opening chapter. It is a question which must arise for any post-positivist philosopher who believes that a sharp distinction can be drawn between truths or reason and truths of fact, and yet who does not want to dismiss all the greatest philosophers as being simply mistaken in what they aimed to do. As will be shown in the next section, it is also a question which must arise for someone who completely denies the positivist's sharp distinction between truths of reason and truths of fact. It is, therefore, a question which must be interesting to anyone interested in the claims, status, and possibilities of philosophy. It is particularly important as a prolegomenon to the present inquiry, which, as an inquiry into what there must be, must assume that it is possible for a philosopher to discover what there must be, and so is, in the world. Answering this question will show both how an inquiry such as the present one might be undertaken and also why it is justified.

§2   It would be natural to think that there should be no real problem about how pure philosophy is possible, or about how philosophers can justifiably describe the world. For it would be natural to assume that it only becomes problematic if the assumption is made that there is an absolute distinction between truths of reason and truths of fact, and that this is a mistaken assumption. Once this distinction is broken down, so also is any distinction between philosophers, or operators

with reason, and scientists, or those dependent also on observation, and so it becomes much more plausible to suppose that
the operations of the one can (and should) have an effect on
the operations of the other.

The claim that this distinction should be weakened has
been particularly connected with the name of Quine. At the
end of *Word and Object,* for example, there is a description
of how puzzles at any level of generality may lead to 'semantic
ascent' and so to those puzzles being treated in a more linguistic and conceptual way. At a certain level people engaging
in such analysis may properly be called philosophers, yet their
work may influence the description of the world which occurs
in the parts of the system most directly related to experience.
On the other hand, they only work with the conceptual
problems that they do because these problems have arisen
from the normal description of such experience. The system
of inquiry, that is, is thought of as continuous, so that philosophical moves can be influenced by description of experience, and
description of experience influenced by philosophical moves.

If the process of inquiry into the nature of the world is
pictured in something like Quine's manner, it is obvious how
philosophers can have an influence on what is decided or
discovered to be in the world. It seems, therefore, to provide
a quick solution to the problem raised in the last section. This
would be a solution by means of elimination, since such a
picture would prevent any possibility of setting the problem
up. For if it is not permitted to have an absolute distinction
between the use of pure reason and the use of observation,
then philosophers and scientists could not be distinguished
from each other in the way in which they were in the last
section, nor could the problem be posed of how someone
could describe the world by the use of pure reason alone. It
seems tempting, therefore, to reject this problem as being
merely an additional worry which arises for post-positivist
philosophers and which need be of no concern to those who
adopt a wiser view about the distinction between truths of
reason and truths of fact.

Although, however, Quine's picture of the nature of inquiry
does provide a way in which people properly called philosophers may influence description of the world, and although
it would prevent the use of the terms in which the problem

posed in the last section was set up, it does not solve the problem of how the great philosophers mentioned at the beginning thought they could describe the world. This is because, on Quine's view, someone working at a highly theoretical level can have influence on description of the world only because all such description is conventional or theory-laden, so that there are always more options open in description than are determined by experience. This is quite explicit in Quine's account of how our knowledge forms a whole, and is expressed as follows in his famous essay 'Two Dogmas of Empiricism':

the totality of our so-called knowledge or beliefs . . . is a man-made fabric which impinges on experience only along the edges . . . conflict with experience at the periphery occasions readjustments in the interior of the field . . . but . . . there is much latitude of choice as to what statements to re-evaluate in the light of any single contrary experience (*From a Logical Point of View*, p. 42).

The philosopher, that is, is permitted interference with the process of description because description is under-determined by experience and so is at the mercy of convention or choice. Yet the conclusions of the great philosophers were not intended merely to influence choice or convention; they were intended, rather, to be true whatsoever the conventions might be. Berkeley thought that he had shown that the inanimate world must consist of ideas, Kant thought that it was causally connected together. Both of them thought themselves to be establishing definitely and finally what was in the actual world, whatever conventions of description might happen to be adopted to describe it.

It is impossible also on the Quinean picture to explain how the problems, arguments, and assumptions of these historically great philosophers can still be understood by philosophers working today. For if knowledge forms a totality in which the philosopher works at a highly theoretical level at problems which arrive by semantic ascent from the slightly less theoretical level of science, then it should not be possible to understand the philosophy of any time without first understanding its science. As science changes, so should philosophy, being provided with different problems, concepts, and assumptions. Yet it is quite obvious that present day philosophers do not need to study large amounts of the history of science in order to be able to criticize the arguments and assumptions of past philosophers. Many of their arguments have a universal appeal, which is independent of particular historical contexts, and so is more in accord with the picture of philosophers working with pure reason alone than with the Quinean picture of their problems arising out of the science of their day.

Although, therefore, a Quinean can provide one sort of explanation of how it is possible that a philosopher can describe the world, he cannot explain how the great philosophers were able to do this, and so he also is faced with some version of the problem raised in the last section. The Quinean depends upon treating what was formerly considered to be a difference of kind as really being a difference of degree. This makes it possible for him to explain how something which is on one side of the line can have influence on something which is on the other, and leads to Quine's unified picture of knowledge in which both highly theoretical and highly experimental inquiries can have influence on each other. They can only have influence on each other, however, by their both having influence on the intermediate links of the continuous chain which joins them, and so the less highly theoretical activity of science must be the means both by which philosophy influences description of the world and also by which philosophical problems arise out of description of the world. It has been seen, however, that in the case of the great philosophers mentioned, neither the ability of philosophers to describe the world nor the source of their problems derives from such a contact between philosophy and this intermediary link in the chain called science. Instead, philosophers seem directly able to describe the world and seem also to start with problems and assumptions which can be understood from generation to generation and are independent of the shifting sands of science or of other conventions in description. This means that the activities of the great philosophers present as large a problem to the Quinean as they do to a post-positivist philosopher. The only difference is that the terms used to pose the problem mark relative rather than absolute distinctions, the problem being now how someone who operates with as pure a use of reason as is possible (who is as near the theoretical end of the scale as possible) can produce descriptions of the nature of the actual world.

There is an additional, purely personal, reason why the normal working philosopher should be interested in the problem raised in the first section even if he is inclined to accept the Quinean view of the nature of the distinction between truths of reason and truths of fact. This is that if the only proper philosophical work involves semantic ascent from the more theoretical science of the day, then it is impossible for someone to work as a philosopher unless he knows a great deal of science. For it is only if someone is in a position where he has the description and theory of one level of abstraction at his fingertips that he can make such a semantic ascent with confidence. Yet few philosophers know that much science and so, if the Quinean picture shows the only way in which philosophers can describe the world, all the others should give up the subject. Those that wish to stay in business, therefore, have an interest in finding an alternative answer to the problem raised in the first section.

§3   So far it has been seen that the great philosophers at least appear to have attempted to describe the actual world by the use of pure reason alone, and that this attempt can neither be dismissed as being based on a simple mistake, nor as an attempt which poses problems only for a post-positivist philosopher. The question must now be faced directly, therefore, of whether and how such an activity might be possible. Can it really be the case that some sort of description of the world is possible without relying on particular observations to originate, or to support, such descriptions? Or are philosophers who attempt to do this just pretenders, only to be supported in the same spirit in which the priests of a national religion might be supported once belief had disappeared in the causal efficacy of their rites, that is for purely historical and picturesque reasons?

If philosophy is a separate and justifiable means of describing the world, independent of science and particular observations, then it must be the case that its results are immune from subsequent discoveries based on science and observation. So, if his activity is to be justified, a philosopher must know prior to observation that his results are immune to refutation by observation. He cannot, therefore, just declare in the way that a scientist can, that certain things are universally so; for he cannot rely in the way that a scientist can on subsequent observation and experiment to bear him out. Instead he must know prior to experience that his results are universally so; and he can only know this if he knows that they are necessarily so. If, then, there is going to be philosophical discovery of the nature of the world, it will not just be a study of how the world is but, rather, a study of how the world must be. This explains why a scientist must go and check up to see if it is as he says it is, for the facts he lays claim to might well be otherwise. It also explains why a philosopher need make no observations, for if he only deals in what must be so, then it is unnecessary for him to go and check whether it actually is so rather than otherwise.

If, therefore, philosophers can inquire into what there must be, they will have an inquiry which may perfectly properly be conducted with the use of pure reason alone, and yet which will tell them about the world. This, however, just seems to make the original problem worse. For it is natural to assume that all necessity comes from the relations between concepts and that from the relations between concepts no conclusions can be validly derived about existents, about how things actually are in the world. It is just this that was held to be wrong with the ontological argument for the existence of God when it was criticized in §1. So if the only way philosophers can operate is by inquiring into what there must be, and the only way necessity can be studied is by examining the relations between concepts, it seems that after all the positivists may have been right and that no study of the world is possible while using pure reason alone.

If negative rather than positive existential conclusions are considered, however, it does not seem so obvious that, even on the purest positivist principles, someone operating with pure reason alone might not be able to describe the world. For although nothing about the world follows from the discovery that two concepts are necessarily connected, it can be found out what does not exist by discovering which concepts are incompatible with one another. We learn nothing about the world, that is, if we discover that the concepts *round* and *circular* are necessarily connected with one another; however,

once we see that the concepts *round* and *square* are incompatible with one another, then we may immediately derive the
existential conclusion that there are no square circles in the
world. This is certainly a conclusion about the world, just
as negative scientific conclusions such as that there is no body
which travels faster than light are conclusions about the
world. It means, for example, that we shall never be confronted with a square circle.

If impossibility is considered instead of necessity, therefore,
it can be seen how, even in accord with the purest positivist
principles, a philosopher may arrive at conclusions about the
actual world. It also helps to illuminate some of the arguments of the great philosophers mentioned at the beginning.
Take, for example, the following passage from Berkeley's
Principles:

For to what purpose is it to dilate on that which may be demonstrated with utmost evidence in a line or two, to any one who is
capable of the least reflection? it is but looking into your own
thoughts, and so trying whether you can conceive it possible for
a sound, or figure, or motion, or colour to exist without the mind,
or unperceived. This easy trial will make you see, that what you
contend for is a downright contradiction (§XXII).

Here it is clear that Berkeley intends to operate by pure
reason alone ('it is but looking into your own thoughts . . .'),
and clear also that he thinks that the conclusion he is aiming
at follows directly from the perception of an incompatibility
between concepts (it is supposed that the alternative position,
in which these concepts are combined, can easily be seen to
be a downright contradiction). Yet the over-all conclusion
to the argument, which is that there cannot be, and so is not,
existence unperceived, is a conclusion about the world. So
Berkeley, of the great philosophers mentioned, does at least
sometimes manage to reach conclusions about the world by
examining incompatibilities between concepts. This is a procedure which has also obviously been used by some philosophers not mentioned at the beginning, for example Plato
and Bradley and, in general, those philosophers of a sceptical
or idealist disposition who wish to show that the world is not
as it appears to be. Common descriptions of the world are
taken by such philosophers and are subjected to ruthless

analysis until they reveal, or at least appear to reveal, hidden contradictions, so showing that, whatever the world is actually like, at least it cannot be as these descriptions represent it as being. This again is a conclusion about the actual world; yet it is one derived solely from analysis of concepts and concentration on impossibilities.

Although, however, concentration on impossibilities does provide a means of solving the original problem of how a philosopher can describe the world, it is neither a sufficiently potent nor a sufficiently certain solution to explain how the great philosophers could describe the world or to provide a method for the present inquiry. It is not sufficiently certain because it relies heavily on the positivist idea of an absolute distinction between the consideration of concepts, which can be conducted by pure reason alone, and the consideration of facts, which requires observation and experiment. Yet it presumably is the case that the concepts are as they are because the facts are as they are; that the concepts we use, that is, have been selected because of their adequacy in describing the facts. If this is the case, and it seems that it is, then consideration of concepts will involve much more covert knowledge of the facts than is permissible for someone who is working by pure reason alone; and will involve much more belief about what the facts are than is appropriate for something which is intended to form a foundation for the present inquiry.

Even if the notion of a concept is better founded and more self-sufficient than this suggests, study of the incompatibilities between concepts would still not be a powerful enough solution to the original problem. It would not explain even the argument quoted above in support and taken from Berkeley. For the weight of Berkeley's argument comes not where he concludes that the position opposed to his own is contradictory, but in the initial steps in which he manoeuvres that alternative position into the contradiction. However, the claim that something more than the notion of bare contradiction is involved in powerful philosophical arguments can perhaps be most clearly demonstrated by the example of Wittgenstein's private language argument. Since the aim of this argument is to show that something is impossible, and since Wittgenstein seems to operate with pure reason alone without placing any particular reliance on observation, it would be natural to expect that the impossibility derived in the conclusion to the argument follows directly from observation of an incompatibility between two concepts. It would be natural to expect, that is, that the argument arrives at its conclusion because it emerges from contemplation of the concept of privacy and the concept of a language that a private language is a contradiction in terms, and so an impossibility. There have been defenders of Wittgenstein who have done just this, arguing that language is by its very nature, by the very meaning of the concept, a public activity. To represent or defend the argument in this way, however, is surely to limit its scope and to fail to do justice to its subtlety. What Wittgenstein's argument does is not to rule out private languages as being a mere contradiction in terms, but to show (or attempt to show) that certain things which we must be able to do in all languages, such as being able to distinguish between what actually is correct and what merely seems to be so, are not things which we would be able to do in a private language.

This example of Wittgenstein's private language argument shows how arguments which might appear to have the form of the proposed solution do not really do so and that, more importantly, such arguments may be much more powerful than an argument in terms of the proposed solution could possibly be. The conclusions to certain philosophical arguments may report the discovery of impossibilities. This, given that a philosopher's conclusions will be about what must be so rather than about what just happens to be so, is only to be expected. It does not mean, however, that these things have been discovered to be impossible just because it has been observed that two concepts are incompatible with each other or that their combination results in a contradiction. The results may be expressed in this way, but the actual argument has gone on elsewhere and is often much more powerful than any argument based just on incompatibilities between concepts could possibly be. It is only by discovering how such more powerful arguments are possible that an adequate answer can be given to the problem raised in the first section of how the great philosophers were able to describe the world, or an adequate foundation given to the inquiry which follows.

§4 It was seen in the last section that if a philosopher is able to discover how the world is by the exercise of pure reason alone, then his discoveries will not be so much about how the world just happens to be as about how the world must necessarily be. It was then seen that this could not be achieved in a satisfactory way by examining either the essential connections or the incompatibilities between concepts, both natural ways of dealing with necessity. The remaining way of attempting to introduce the required element of necessity is by means of a hypothetical, showing that something is necessary if something else is to be the case or is to be achieved. To take again the previous example, it was seen that no conclusions of a categorical form about how the world actually is follow from the realization that the concepts *round* and *circular* are essentially connected with one another. It is obvious, however, that a hypothetical conclusion about the nature of the world may perfectly properly follow from this realization. This is the conclusion that if there are circular things in the world then there are round things in it.

The propriety of such a conclusion is obvious, and would be admitted by the most absolute post-positivist. Unfortunately it again seems to provide no help with the general problem of how a philosopher may describe the world. For it seems that no categorical conclusions about how the world actually is could be derived from this kind of hypothetical statement unless it was known that the state of affairs described in the protasis of the hypothetical actually obtained in the world. It would have to be known, for example, that there actually were circular things in the world in order to make use of the hypothetical conclusion just given. Yet if such further particular information about the world is needed in order to apply such hypothetical statements, it seems that a philosopher could not use such statements in an attempt to find out what was in the world. For if the philosopher works with pure reason alone, it seems that he could have no access to the required pieces of particular information or knowledge about the world.

However, although considering hypothetical statements does not seem to help in solving the original problem of how someone operating with pure reason alone can describe the world, it does show how such a person may be able to arrive at useful and interesting results about the world. For he may be able to arrive at hypothetical conclusions showing the interesting and unforeseen consequences of certain things being the case about the world. This will not by itself enable him to declare that these interesting consequences describe how the world actually is. If however the particular bits of information which he needs, in order to know that the protases of his hypothetical statements are satisfied are extremely obvious or agreed, then he can show that these obvious or agreed facts involve certain other interesting or important things being true about the world. Starting with given information, that is, the philosopher may be able to derive new and surprising results about how the world is. If the information that he starts with is extremely obvious or undisputed, and the conclusions he derives are relatively unobvious or disputed, he will have performed a valuable service in showing how the world is while operating with nothing but pure reason.

The hypothetical form of conclusion, and the demonstration that certain unforeseen or disputed conclusions about the world follow from obvious or readily assumed facts about how things are, can both be illustrated by the conclusion of Kant's mentioned at the beginning. This is the conclusion that the changes in the objects of the world have to be causally connected together. At first sight this looks like a straightforward categorical conclusion about the nature of the actual world. Kant arrives at this conclusion, however, because he assumes that the world is such that we can have empirical knowledge about it. So it would be more accurate to put his result in the form of a hypothetical, saying that if we are going to have empirical knowledge of a world then that world must consist of objects causally connected together. This means that his conclusions are not strictly speaking directly about the world unless the separate piece of information that the world is such that we can have knowledge of it is either assumed or supposed to be known on other grounds. Yet, at least compared to Kant's conclusion, this is a relatively agreed and obvious piece of information about the world. So Kant's argument can be said to perform the valuable service of showing what unobvious and important conclusions necessarily follow from such an obvious and agreed piece of information.

This example from Kant suggests how philosophers can

describe the world. Since the conclusion is in a hypothetical form there is no direct production of facts by pure reason alone. The procedure, therefore, should be satisfactory even in positivist or post-positivist eyes, since no conclusions are derived about the world unless some facts about the world are already assumed or known. Yet Kant shows that it is important which facts or information need to be known or assumed in this way. It is important that these are relatively obvious or agreed, or that there is something else about them that makes their assumption justified. The more obvious they are, the more important the job is that a philosopher performs when he derives their consequences. For the more obvious they are, the less reliance needs to be placed on things that cannot be discovered by pure reason alone. Ideally, the philosopher would have to work only with assumptions about the world which were so obvious or certain that he could quite justifiably assume them without any particular use of fact or observation. If it is the case that there are certain things about how the world is that may be assumed in this way, then the philosopher should concentrate on deriving their consequences. In this way he can work with pure reason alone (for no particular observation of, or knowledge about, the world will be required either for his initial assumptions or for drawing the consequences of these assumptions) and yet he will be able to arrive at conclusions about the actual world.

The problem of how philosophers are able to describe the world, then, is only partially illuminated by reference to the hypothetical form of conclusion and comes down centrally to the problem of whether there are any assumptions about how the world is that may properly be made by someone operating with pure reason alone. This can be seen by comparing the way that a philosopher (Kant for example) can talk about the world with the way that someone who knows the connections of concepts expressed in simple arithmetic can talk about the world. For a piece of simple arithmetic can also be represented as a hypothetical conclusion about the actual world; this is the form, for example, of the following statement: 'If there are 22 things in one half of something and 12 things in the other half of the same thing, then there are 34 things in it altogether.' Given certain information about the world, for example that there are 22 oranges in the left hand side of a box and 12 oranges in the right hand side, this would enable someone to derive by pure reason alone that there were 34 oranges in the whole box. As in Kant's case, once certain information about the world is possessed, then the results of hypothetical statements can be used to obtain further information about the world. So reference to the hypothetical form of conclusion places Kant's discoveries in the same place as the conclusions of arithmetic. The difference between them comes not in the form but in the nature of the extra information that is needed in order to apply these hypothetical conclusions to the world. For in the arithmetical example, the extra information that is needed is obviously highly specific and could only be obtained by particular observation or deductions based on particular observations. It obviously could not be obtained by the use of pure reason alone. In Kant's case, however, the only further information that needs to be assumed is that the world is such that we can have empirical knowledge about it. This is quite a general assumption, not depending upon particular knowledge of fact or observation, and one therefore which would much more naturally be assumed by someone wishing to discover the nature of the world using pure reason alone. The difference between the cases, therefore, comes in the difference in the extra information or assumptions required, and the heart of the general problem is the problem of whether there are any assumptions about the nature of the world which may justifiably be made by someone using pure reason alone. This is the problem which will be examined in the next section.

There is an additional reason why it is important to notice that the extra information or assumptions which are needed in order to apply philosophical conclusions to the world are quite different from the information which is needed to apply the equally hypothetical conclusions of mathematics or logic. This is that if the assumption or assumptions used are selected because they are just those which may justifiably be assumed by someone using pure reason alone, they will obviously play a central part in the subsequent argument. For if it is only the consequences of such assumptions that can properly or usefully be drawn by the philosopher, then it is important that he knows which assumptions these are before he starts work drawing consequences. This makes his situation very different from the one of the pure mathematician or logician who may happily connect together the concepts involved in his work without bothering about whether the protases of his conclusions, if they were cast in hypothetical form, would be satisfied. It means that the extra assumptions used by a philosopher will be few, centrally important, and will have a dominating effect on the course of his argument; whereas the extra assumptions required in order to apply the conclusions of a mathematician or logician to the world will be many, will be unconsidered by him, and will have no effect on the course of his argument.

This difference has a great advantage in the strength of philosophical arguments that can be produced. Since a philosopher is concerned with the necessary conditions for, and the essential consequences of, a few particular assumptions, he need not at any stage in his argument be concerned just with the way that the concepts he uses are essentially connected together in themselves but only needs to consider which things are essential for each other if one of these assumptions is to be satisfied. This means that he is not restricted just to the consideration of logical necessities nor to the production of the kind of arguments that can be produced by the sheer contemplation of concepts alone. A philosopher, therefore, is able to produce arguments of greater power than would be possible if he just examined the interconnection of concepts or (to put it in a less positivist way) the more conceptual areas of inquiry. This marks another difference between philosophical argument and other types of argument that proceed by pure reason alone, and one which offers hope of someone being able to discover interesting and important conclusions while using philosophical argument. It shows that if certain assumptions can be found which it is justifiable to assume while operating with pure reason alone, then these assumptions will not only be important in the application of philosophical conclusions to the world, but will also be important to dictating the scope and course of the philosophical argument itself, and in controlling the power of conclusion that can be reached by the argument.

§5   Solution of the central problem of this chapter has now been narrowed down to the problem of whether there are any assumptions about the nature of the world which it would be justifiable for someone to make who was operating with pure reason alone. At first sight this just seems to make the problem as intractable as ever, for it seems quite obvious that nothing might have existed at all, and if nothing might have existed at all then it must be purely contingent whether any particular thing, or particular kind of thing, exists or not. There is nothing, as was remarked in §1 in connection with the ontological argument for the existence of God, of which it can be said that it necessarily exists. So it seems that all conclusions, facts, and assumptions about the nature of the world must be based on particular observation and that it cannot be told by pure reason alone that anything at all exists, let alone any particular kind of thing.

The present problem or question, however, is not that of showing by pure reason alone that something exists. It is, rather, the question of whether it is justifiable to assume the existence of anything, or justifiable to assume in any way how the world is, if an attempt is being made to discover the nature of the world by pure thought alone. This is a situation in which we have someone thinking about the world, and now it does seem that there are certain assumptions that it is proper for him to make, for example that he is thinking about the world. Here the force of Descartes's *cogito* argument becomes apparent. Although it is purely contingent whether any philosopher exists or not, just as it is purely contingent whether anything at all exists or not, once a philosopher is thinking about these problems, then it seems justifiable for him to assume that he is thinking about these problems, or at least that he is thinking, or that there is thought going on.

Descartes's *cogito* argument provides a start in suggesting the kind of assumptions that it might be justifiable for someone to make who was operating with pure reason alone. For it reminds us that although anything or nothing might exist, these are all situations which we as philosophers are thinking about. If, for example, we think that we might not have existed, this is to think of the situation from the point of view of someone else who does exist and has never seen anything else appear which looks like us. We imagine, that is, someone describing the whole world (everything that exists) and us not being included in that description. Similarly, if we think that nothing existed at one time or that nothing exists at all, we do this by imagining (*per impossibile*) some kind of god outside the whole system who saw nothing at the time in question, or who sees nothing whatsoever. Considering such situations is first of all to bring them into relation with our own thought and secondly to connect them with the possibility of someone else's perception of them (or of our own perception in different circumstances). However, if this is the case, any conditions there are on thought or perception will apply to these situations. Either, that is, these sort of situations can not be considered or studied at all (in which case they could be of no possible interest to us), or else they are situations which it must be possible to think of and situations which can be brought into relation with perception. So any situation which can be considered or studied, any situation in which we could be interested, is a situation which fulfils any conditions which there may be on thought or perception.

Take, for example, the situation in which nothing at all exists. Although it is possible that the present situation could have been like this (for it is contingent whether anything exists or not), it is not possible for us, who are doing the considering, to think that our present situation actually is like this. For we have to exist in order to consider; and so something exists. We can, of course, consider what it would have been like if nothing existed. But this is to consider what might have been the case, not to consider what might actually be the case. It is to examine how things might have been, not how they are. If we are considering the present, actual, situation, therefore, it is a fair assumption that something actually does exist. For if nothing existed we could have no interest at all in the situation. The possibility that nothing exists, that is, can neither be considered nor referred to in any way unless it does not occur. So even though it is logically possible that nothing exists, it is justifiable to assume, purely *a priori* and independently of observation, that something does exist. For we could have no interest whatsoever in the situation in which this assumption does not hold.

The assumption that something exists is only one example of an assumption which, although it is existential, may perfectly justifiably be assumed by someone operating with pure reason alone. Another example is the assumption that what exists is such that we are able to judge and describe it. For, again, although it is logically possible that what exists is such that we could not judge or describe it, it would be impossible for us to consider or describe any situation for which this assumption did not apply. Again, we are either left with a situation in which we could have no possible interest, or else the assumption must be made. Here, then, is another assumption which it would be justifiable for someone operating with pure reason alone to make.

This second suggested assumption is exactly the kind of assumption that is required to apply a philosopher's conclusions to the world, and in the light of which interesting and important arguments can be generated in the manner suggested at the end of the last section. It is the assumption that there exists a world which can be thought about, or that there exists a world which can be comprehended. It is justifiable for a philosopher to assume it without benefit of particular knowledge or observation for he, like anybody else, can have neither theoretical nor practical interest in a world which could not be judged or comprehended. Once he has made this assumption he can then work out the essential conditions of a world being judged or being comprehensible. He will find in this way which things must be the case about a world if it is to be comprehensible and so find, assuming that the world is comprehensible, what the world is like. Yet in doing all this he will be operating with pure reason alone.

Here, then, is a solution to the central problem of this chapter. If the philosopher considers the essential conditions of a world being a comprehensible one he will work with pure reason alone and yet will arrive at conclusions about the actual world since it is justifiable to assume that the world is a comprehensible one and so to apply his conclusions (which would otherwise be hypothetical) to the actual world. This solution, therefore, provides both motive and justification for the kind of inquiry which this book is centrally concerned with. This is an inquiry into the essential conditions of a world being a comprehensible one. It is an inquiry into what there must be in any comprehensible world. According to choice, its results can be left in hypothetical form or else applied to the actual world by means of the justifiable additional assumption that this world is a comprehensible one.

This inquiry begins in the next chapter. Before then, the present chapter ends with an historical note on the method just proposed as solution to the problem with which it started, with consideration of an important objection to the use of this method at all, and with provision of further reasons why the present inquiry should be undertaken.

§6   The solution proposed in the last section to the general problem of this chapter is essentially that of Kant. Kant was interested in producing a method of philosophical inquiry which would enable him to argue in an *a priori* manner (that is, by using pure reason alone) about what the world is like without merely connecting together concepts in the way that is attempted, for example, in the Ontological Argument for the existence of God. By attacking such a procedure he broke away from his philosophical past and from his German predecessors, Wolff and Leibniz. However, he was equally dissatisfied with the empiricist alternative as put forward, in different ways, by Locke and by Hume, since this alternative seemed to result in complete scepticism about the possibility of putting forward any account from the *a priori* position of what the world is like. Kant discovered a third way between these two alternatives which could be put in over simple terms as that, if the understanding could not have knowledge *a priori* of the world, it could still have knowledge *a priori* of itself and so have knowledge *a priori* of what it was possible for it to know. Although, therefore, the understanding could not say directly what the world was like, it could say directly what any world would have to be like if it were to be understood and known, if it were to be comprehended.

The manner in which this discovery of Kant's has been described uses his own over-concrete terminology in which the mind is divided into separate entities such as the understanding and the sensibility. However, it is clear that Kant's third way is very similar to the solution adopted in the last section to the general problem of this chapter. Kant may, that is, be held to have discovered the method in philosophy which has emerged as an answer to this problem and which will be adopted in the inquiry which follows. He sums up this discovery in the following famous passage which appears in the preface to the second edition of the *Critique of Pure Reason*:

Hitherto it has been assumed that all our knowledge must conform
to objects. But all attempts to extend our knowledge of objects
by establishing something in regard to them *a priori*, by means
of concepts, have, on this assumption, ended in failure. We must
therefore make trial whether we may not have more success in
the tasks of metaphysics, if we suppose that objects must conform
to our knowledge. This would agree better with what is desired,
namely, that it should be possible to have knowledge of objects
a priori, determining something in regard to them prior to their
being given. We should then be proceeding precisely on the lines
of Copernicus' primary hypothesis. Failing of satisfactory progress
in explaining the movements of the heavenly bodies on the supposition that they all revolved around the spectator, he tried
whether he might not have better success if he made the spectator
to revolve and the stars to remain at rest. A similar experiment can
be tried in metaphysics, as regards the *intuition* of objects. If
intuition must conform to the constitution of the objects, I do
not see how we could know anything of the latter *a priori*; but
if the object (as object of the senses) must conform to the constitution of our faculty of intuition, I have no difficulty in conceiving
such a possibility (Bxvi–xvii).

The images and analogies employed in this passage, particularly the famous comparison with Copernicus, are again misleading if the argument of this passage is taken to be describing
the kind of inquiry that is going to be followed in this book.
For this passage has obvious idealist tendencies, implying that
the understanding can know the world because the world
depends upon the understanding, or that the world is as it
is because the understanding is as it is. This is not an assumption of the present inquiry, and in the next section it will be
shown that it is quite permissible to adopt the Kantian style
of argument without adopting his idealism.

Since Kant may be held to have invented or discovered the
kind of argument used in this inquiry, Kant's own name for it
is usually adopted, and such arguments are usually called
transcendental ones. Kant contrasted 'transcendental' with
'transcendent'; by 'transcendent' he meant the bad old metaphysics that he was attempting to destroy, the metaphysics
that attempted to argue about how the world is by a mere connection of concepts, the metaphysics that rested on the idea
that reason transcended or went beyond experience, so that,
for example, it was claimed that we could know by reason

alone about the real world of Platonic ideas or, by the onto-logical argument, God. In contrast Kant used 'transcendental' (although he was not completely consistent in his use of this pair of terms) to describe *a priori* argument which did not seek to transcend experience or empirical knowledge, but which related to the possibility of there being experience or knowledge at all. It is concerned, therefore, not so much with the objects themselves as with our knowledge of them. In Kant's own words: 'I entitle transcendental all knowledge which is occupied not so much with objects as with the mode of our knowledge of objects in so far as this mode is to be possible *a priori*' (B25).

These transcendental arguments provide a richer and more powerful way of arguing about what is in the world while using pure reason alone than would be possible if one just had to rely on relaxing the distinction between truths of reason and truths of fact in the way that was considered in §2, or looking for contradictions in description, as considered in §3. This can be shown by a sketchy picture of one way in which Kant can be taken to reply to Hume. Hume considered and was concerned with logical connections. He realized, quite correctly, that there are no such connections between matters of fact, so that how things have happened at one time and place does not entail anything about how things happen at another time or place. Yet this is to look at things from an external, god-like position in which no concern is given to how or whether the things mentioned can be known or des-cribed. It is just assumed, that is, that whatever there is can be known or described, and that it can therefore be seen how the descriptions of the various parts of the world are logically separate from one another. In the same way, or from the same sort of position, it could be seen that it was logically possible that nothing whatever existed or that whatever did exist was completely incomprehensible.

Kant did not deny these Humean conclusions, which are all, as far as they go, quite correct. However, he realized that these conclusions overlook one problem about the situations which they declare to be possible, and this is how it could ever be known that we were in such a situation. Kant, it might be said, realized that all situations in which we could be inter-ested, all situations which could be objects of knowledge for

us, are situations in which it would be possible for us to
understand or judge them. This means that the situations can
no longer be described from an external, god-like position
in which no concern is taken about how such description
is possible. Instead, it is possible to discover certain conditions which must be met by any situation which it would
be possible for us, or for someone like us, to describe or
to understand. When these conditions are discovered they
may show that it is not possible for us to consider some of
the situations Hume has shown to be logically possible to be
real possibilities, to be worlds which we ourselves could be
in.

For example, suppose it to be the case that one such condition can be discovered to be that description of the objects
in the world must be connected together in some way, so that
how things are described at one time or place is not completely independent of how they are described at another
time or place. Then Kant's reply to Hume could be put as
follows. Hume is perfectly correct in pointing out that from a
strictly logical point of view there is no connection between
descriptions made at one time or place and descriptions made
at another time or place. However, once the conditions on the
possibility of description, and so on the possibility of comprehensible experience, are considered, the situation alters. For
then it is discovered (it is supposed) that it would be impossible for us to comprehend a world in which there was not
some connection between descriptions. This means that
although Hume is right that the whole world might become
inextricably confusing tomorrow, or even cease to exist
altogether, if either of these situations were to come about then
the world could no longer be a world for us. As long, therefore, as the world is to continue being a world for us (that is,
a world we can describe and in which we can be interested),
it must be a world in which there is some connection between
descriptions even though there is no question of any entail-
ments holding between these descriptions.

This very hasty sketch of how Kant could be taken to reply
to Hume, while it is obviously too general to serve as any
proper kind of historical sketch, may help to show how Kant's
third way can be used to develop interesting and powerful
arguments about how the world is. It indicates the kind of

conclusion which the following inquiry can hope to attain, and shows that the credit for the discovery of the kind of argument to be used properly belongs to Kant.

§7   Kant himself was clearly an idealist, and the picture he gives of his enterprise in the passage quoted at length in the last section is most naturally taken in an idealist way. For it looks as if Kant asserts that after seeing that he could not know *a priori* what objects there are if the mind depends upon these objects, he sees he could know what objects there are if the objects depended on the mind. This is the natural way to take the analogy with Copernicus and yet, of course, if what the objects of knowledge are is held to depend upon the nature of the mind that knows them, then these objects can only exist in an ideal way. However, a solution to the general problem of this chapter which involves idealism cannot be acceptable, since this problem was just the problem of how someone could by the application of reason alone know the independent, actual world.

If transcendental arguments essentially involve idealism, therefore, they cannot form the solution to the general problem considered in this chapter. Yet this is just what the example of Kant would seem to indicate, and Professor B. A. O. Williams, for example, writing in the *Philosophical Review* for 1968, claims that recent interpreters of Kant who consider his arguments to be similar to ones they themselves want to use 'perhaps pay insufficient attention to Kant's insistence that his transcendental arguments give knowledge of how things must be only because the things are not things in themselves. The idealism was what was supposed to make the whole enterprise possible' (p. 218). It is obviously natural, therefore, to suppose that transcendental arguments essentially involve idealism, and the claim that they do could be put as that, if we can find out what there is by finding out how we must think, this can only be because we have assumed that what there is depends on what we think, rather than assuming that what we think depends on what there is, which is to assume idealism rather than realism.

In spite of such a strong appearance to the contrary, however, idealism is not an essential assumption for the use of transcendental arguments. Finding out the conditions which any world must fulfil in order to be a comprehensible world does not involve any idealist assumption, since it does not involve the assumption that anything that there is depends upon the understanding. It is finding out, rather, what conditions must be met by what exists independently of the understanding if that thing is to be comprehended. In transcendental arguments, that is, we find out what the world is like by studying the understanding. This, however, is not because it is assumed that what there is depends on the understanding (which would be an idealist assumption) but, rather, because it can be assumed that the world which exists independently of us is an understandable one. This is the assumption that it was claimed in §5 might justifiably be assumed while using pure reason alone, and whose operation was illustrated in a sketchy way in the last section. Yet it is not an assumption which involves idealism for it is an assumption which is made about the real world which exists independently of our thought and understanding. To assume that the world is understandable is quite different from assuming that it depends upon the understanding; only the latter assumption involves idealism, yet only the former need be made while using transcendental arguments.

Although, therefore, Kant provides an example of the kind of argument to be used in the inquiry which follows, he gives a misleading impression of how such arguments operate. He is right in seeing that we can find out how the world is, while using pure reason alone not by studying it directly in itself, but by turning our attention to the medium through which alone it can be known to us. By turning our attention from the object itself to the relation it has with us, we can discover which properties the object must possess. Assuming, that is, that the object is comprehensible, we can find out what its properties are by finding out what the essential conditions of any object being a comprehensible object are. Kant, however, is wrong in thinking that the object only has these properties because it is comprehended by us; in thinking that these properties are added by its relation to us and are not possessed by the object in itself. It is not necessary for the use of transcendental arguments that the properties discovered by the use of these arguments are thought of as being added to the object by its relation to a comprehending subject. It may perfectly properly be assumed for the use of such arguments, and it will be assumed in the inquiry which follows, that the object in itself is comprehensible to us and that it possesses the properties it is discovered to have whether or not it is being comprehended by us. The properties in question, that is, are not added to the object by its relation with us. Rather, because it is assumed that the object has this relation, it is known that the object must possess those properties which are essential if such a relation is to be possible. In spite of the impression given by Kant's use of these arguments, therefore, there is not after all an essential connection between the use of transcendental arguments and an assumption of idealism.

§8   Even if it is thought that this chapter has succeeded in establishing the possibility of someone discovering the nature of the world by pure reason alone, it might still be wondered why anyone should bother to do this. For it seems that any conclusions reached in this way about the actual world will be much less particular and much less useful than conclusions about the world reached by the more normal process of observation or empirical science. So if a philosopher is just trying to say by pure reason how the world is to help himself in the common and pragmatic business of day-to-day living, as a scientist at least partly is, then it would seem that he was using an obviously inefficient method.

The reason why someone should bother finding out how the world is while using pure reason alone is not, however, because it might provide an alternative method of finding food or shelter, or of providing means for manipulating the environment. The reason is, rather, the special form of certainty or security that attaches to the results of such an inquiry. It is not, that is, that more things can be known but, rather, that they can be known in a particular way and so be immune from certain kinds of doubt. Conclusions about the world which are reached by pure reason alone can be used as an answer to sceptical arguments about what is in the world in a way that conclusions based on knowledge of particular facts or observation can never be. Observation cannot be used in answer to these arguments since their whole point is to undermine confidence in observation, and it cannot be told by observation alone that observation is trustworthy. Solipsistic arguments, for example, allow for, and explain, the fact that there appear to be other people in the world. So they cannot be refuted by apparent observations of other people. They can, however, be refuted if it can be shown by pure reason alone that there must be other people in the world.

Even though they both describe the actual world, therefore, this sort of philosophy is not in conflict with science. The purpose of the two sorts of description is quite different. Philosophy cannot rival science and common observation in producing an account of the world sufficient for the everyday business of living, and should not attempt to do so. On the other hand, science and common observation cannot answer certain notorious sceptical arguments, and these can only be answered by the kind of conclusions about the actual world that can be produced by philosophy. These sceptical arguments are worth refuting if only because they have been produced by the application of normal thought to their respective subject matters. Yet if thinking about these subjects has produced such apparently paradoxical results and such mental tangles, then anyone who believes in thinking at all must believe that thinking can untie the tangles and remove the paradoxes. It may be the philosophers themselves who have raised the dust, but this just makes it all the more important for philosophers to lay it again. The notorious sceptical arguments are a slur on the intellect and must be refuted with equally powerful arguments before the intellect is cleared of suspicion. Otherwise it would be better just to act and not to think at all, which would be the end of science as well as the end of philosophy.

Anyone who values the processes of thought or the possibilities of the intellect, therefore, must have an interest in refuting these sceptical arguments. This would seem sufficient justification for an inquiry such as the following which, among other things, does precisely this. However, for those who still think that this part of philosophy is merely (in Bradley's phrase) the production of bad reasons for what is believed on instinct, there is an independent, and perhaps more important, reason why a philosopher should attempt to work out how the world is by the use of pure reason alone. This is that the normal processes of empirical science and common observation produce different results at different

times, in different circumstances, and according to different
cultures. This is an age of relativism, and it is no longer possible to measure philosophical conclusions against the unques-
tionable dictates of common sense. Changes of fashion in
anthropology, the Sapir–Whorf theory in linguistics and
Quine's theoretical defence of it in his examination of the
indeterminancy of translation (*Word and Object*, Ch. 2) have
all combined to give the unquestioned assumptions of one
language or culture a relative rather than an absolute
authority in deciding how things actually are. An index of
this change can be seen in the increase of interest in the
history of thought and the history of science, which in its
turn leads to further undermining of the belief that the
science of any particular time is the final authority as to how
things actually are. There is confidence about the question
of what existential assumptions are made by various conceptual schemes, but there is no confidence about the question
of what there is *simpliciter*. In such a situation there is an
obvious and important role for an inquiry which can tell by
pure reason alone, and without relying on the basic factual
assumptions employed by various cultures or conceptual
schemes, how things are in the world. The same confusion of
doctrines as existed in the Renaissance and can be seen exemplified, for example, in Montaigne is with us again, and now
as then the answer seems to be to return to the resources of
pure reason alone.

  The same move from a single certainty of doctrine to a
complex multiplicity of positions and relativism in assertion
can be seen in the recent history of positivism, for example
from Schlick to Feyerabend. In the beginning there was an
absolute, single, and relatively simple means of distinguishing
between the assertions about how things were which could be
accepted as significant, and the assertions about how things
were which had to be dismissed as meaninglessness. All significant statements were significant in the same way and formed
part of a unitary language of science. The positivist tradition
ends up in the completely opposite position in which all assertions have equal right, are all justified from their own point
of view, and so are all mutually incomprehensible. Witch-
burning puritanism has gradually transformed itself into
licentious and mutually unheeding babel. Although most

people would agree with the original movement away from the single-voiced and austere doctrine with its one criterion of acceptability, most people do not wish to follow this movement to its natural end with as many voices as there are people and with no criteria at all by which to distinguish between acceptable and unacceptable judgements. Most people want some kind of control, some kind of standards that judgements have to match up to if they are going to be thought of as judgements about the world. Such standards will be produced by the following inquiry into the essential conditions of any world being a comprehensible world. Any necessary conditions that are found will provide some check on the ramifying multiplicity of doctrines, and will provide a standard that judgements in any language or system will have to match up to if they can be considered acceptable. If we can tell by pure reason alone how the world is, this means that we do not need to treat all conceptual schemes on a par without any attempt to discriminate between them. If we can establish by pure reason alone certain necessary conditions which must be fulfilled by any judgement which is to be a judgement about the world, then it is possible to distinguish between judgements and hold that certain of them cannot be judgements about the world.

It is important to tell by pure reason alone, then, how the world is so that certain sceptical arguments can be answered and certain sceptical doubts laid. Since the arguments have been produced by reason, it is important if reason is going to be considered trustworthy that they can also be answered by reason. This might, however, seem to be rather an intellectual game, were it not that the diversity of beliefs and conceptual schemes provides a real ground for doubts about the possibility of finding out what there is. Since relying on common sense and common judgement is no longer considered completely dependable in producing more than a relative answer, it is important that some method can be discovered of finding out what there is, or at least of establishing necessary conditions which must be met by any attempt to say what there is. This method, the production of conclusions about the world by pure reason alone, is what the following inquiry provides.

CHAPTER TWO

Method of Inquiry

§9 REDUCTION VERSUS CONSTRUCTION

IN the last chapter the general problem was considered of how a philosopher might be able to describe the world. Even though it seemed at first sight that no one who operated with pure reason alone and independently of particular experiences or observations could properly claim to be discovering the nature of the world, it emerged in §§4 and 5 both that such a person might perfectly properly consider the essential consequences of certain assumptions and also that there were indeed assumptions which might quite properly be made from the *a priori* position which such a person occupies. One of these was that it could be assumed, or presupposed, that the world was such that it was possible to make judgements about it or to describe it. It is proper to assume, that is, that there exists a world which can be judged or comprehended; and that the philosopher can discover the nature of this world by discovering the essential conditions of a world being a comprehensible one. The following inquiry proceeds on this assumption and is, accordingly, an inquiry into the essential conditions of any world being a comprehensible one; or an inquiry into the fundamental features of any comprehensible conceptual scheme.

This inquiry, of course, does not depend upon the arguments and conclusions of Chapter One. It might quite properly be conducted by someone who disagreed completely with Chapter One and, by showing what are the fundamental features of any world which can be thought about, be used to discover something about the nature of our thought. With the additional premiss that our present world is a comprehensible one, it could also be used to discover certain very general features of this world. However, even if the arguments of Chapter One are not essential for the inquiry, they do give it a particular importance and point by demonstrating that this additional premiss is not an arbitrary extra but, on the contrary, an assumption which may perfectly properly be made from the *a priori* point of view.

The inquiry which follows, then, is an inquiry into the fundamental features of any comprehensible conceptual scheme, or into the essential conditions which must be met by any world which can be thought about or judged. It will start by assuming a few very central and essential features which must be possessed by any world which can be comprehended. The consequences and preconditions of these features will then be investigated, so showing which other features are essential. These features, in turn, will yield still further features by examination of their consequences and preconditions. In this way a complete picture of all the essential features can be constructed.

Many attempts to discover the more central or essential features of our present conceptual scheme do not use a constructive method like this one, which involves starting with just a few essential features and building up a complete picture of all the fundamental features which are required. Instead, they employ reductive methods which work much nearer the surface of our present conceptual scheme, and which endeavour to isolate the more essential parts of it by stripping off the superfluous features. One form of this method, for example, is the device of mapping the whole of our conceptual scheme on to a part of itself, in order to show that the part not included is theoretically dispensable and not as fundamental as the part that remains. Such a device is used by Strawson in *Individuals*, both in his construction of a world of sounds ('How far can we map the structure of this whole within a part of itself?' (p. 63)), and also when trying to frame a language without particulars ('We must find some surrogate, in the conceptual materials we are allowed, for these features of the conceptual materials we are not allowed' (p. 218)).

Such a device, however, could not be used without a prior idea about which features of the situation are to be regarded as more fundamental and which as less. For every feature of the part we are attempting to dispense with cannot be mapped on the rest of the system, since this would be in fact to reintroduce it. Only certain features of the eliminated part can be mapped on to the rest, and so whether a particular mapping is possible or not will depend on a decision about what those features are to be. Reduction by means of mapping, therefore, can only take place if there is a prior idea about which features are going to be regarded as more essential. Strawson, for example, has such a prior idea of which features he regards as more essential when considering the possibility of the sounds world since he aims to make it a world in which it is possible to draw a distinction between states of oneself and states not of oneself, and so obviously regards this as an essential feature of any world.

The same consideration applies to an alternative form of the stripping off method, Quine's technique of paraphrase. Quine does not consider his paraphrases to be synonymous. He says, rather, that they preserve those functions of the expressions paraphrased 'that make it worth troubling about' (*Word and Object*, p. 258). He considers a paraphrase good 'insofar as it tends to meet needs for which the original might be wanted' (p. 182). However, it is again the case that unless a prior decision has been made about which needs are more important or about what makes an expression worth troubling about, then attempting a paraphrase would be the impossible task of paraphrasing a description of the whole of something (for example the conceptual scheme) into successively more limited parts of itself. Unless a prior decision about the relative importance of the parts of the conceptual scheme under review has already been made there can be no paraphrasing; and such decision involves use of the other, or building up, method.

This means that the reductive method cannot be used without use, either overt or covert, of the constructive method. For unless a prior decision is made about which features are more essential, then a reductive method such as mapping or paraphrase cannot be used at all; and it is just such decisions which constitute the constructive, or building up, method. Whichever method is employed, prior decisions have to be made about which features are more essential. However, such decisions are naturally part of a constructive method and form its first premises or assumptions. This means that the features selected are extremely fundamental or essential, and that construction can proceed from them in an organized and orderly way. Whereas when such decisions are employed in order to use a reductive method, the features which are selected as essential are done so in an arbitrary and *ad hoc* manner. This arbitrariness can only be avoided if previous, extensive use of the constructive method has been employed in order to demonstrate that the features presumed to be essential for the purpose of a particular mapping or paraphrase really are essential. This is why the constructive method is the one employed in the following inquiry; certain extremely fundamental features will be assumed as being essential in any comprehensible world and the other features will be derived from them.

§10 NEURATH'S SHIP

In the last section it was argued that the inquiry should start at an extremely fundamental level and build up a picture of the essential features of any comprehensible world starting with just a few primitive parts. It might seem that this proposed starting-point was impossible in that it involved the study of an extremely primitive world or conceptual scheme without presupposing any other world or conceptual scheme whatsoever. Whereas it seems that worlds, like anything else, can only be studied inside the context of a fully-fledged language or conceptual scheme. In particular, it could be argued, the starting point must be with our present world and language. This is assumed by Quine, for example, at the beginning of *Word and Object*, and is one of the motives for his adoption of a reductive procedure. He compares the philosopher's situation with the scientist's situation described by Neurath in which the scientist has to rebuild his ship plank by plank in the open sea (*Word and Object*, p. 3).

This analogy of Neurath's expresses particularly well the feeling that any start must be made with where we are at present and so with, or in the context of, our present world. It is quite true that the rebuilding of a ship at sea is a slow and delicate process in which after any particular move the whole is left in much the same condition. Suppose, however, that someone did not wish to rebuild the ship, but just wished to see what could be built, that he just wished to see what the ship could be like or could have been like. This could be achieved while the ship was at sea by building model ships inside itself. Such model ships would show how very different the ship could be or could have been and yet be able to float. They could also be used to show what must be in common to all ships that are able to float.

If this analogy is applied to the question of how it is possible to examine very different or very primitive conceptual schemes, then it can be seen that it is possible to examine how different a world could have been, and yet be comprehensible by the device of building it as a model world inside the context of our present world. The requirement that such a world must satisfy (analogous to the requirement that the model ship should be able to float) is that it should be comprehensible to someone on the inside of itself, a person who may conveniently be labelled the protagonist of that world. This may be achieved, however, without changing the present world at all, but merely by the device of building a model world. Since it is only a model world that is being built, it is possible to start at an extremely fundamental level, for it need not possess enough materials to make it comprehensible at the beginning any more than a model ship need be able to float at the start of its building. Yet once the model world is developed enough to be comprehensible to its protagonist, then it provides a model of a world that could have stood by itself. The device of model worlds, therefore, enables an extremely fundamental start to be made while allowing that we always have to work within the context of our present and complex conceptual scheme.

Of course both the example of Neurath's ship and also its suggested extension in terms of model ships are metaphors. They replace questions about conceptual schemes with questions about one kind of particular concrete object. However, even though it is the extension of a metaphor, the suggestion about building model ships does show how it is possible to study the essential conditions for some property of our conceptual scheme (its comprehensibility) without changing it or having to use a method that depends upon it in more than a methodological way. For this may be done in the same way as a property of a ship we are travelling in (its ability to float) may be studied without having to change the ship itself. In both cases, inside the context of the present situation, extremely different and fundamental situations can be studied. In both cases construction of alternatives is possible which begins at such a fundamental level, but which does not involve changing the present situation in any way.

Since this is a useful analogy, the inquiry which follows can be thought of as the construction of a model world in the context of the present situation, a model world which is comprehensible to its protagonist. Construction of this model world can start at an extremely fundamental level by assuming some feature which is essential in any comprehensible world. The other features which are presupposed by, or which follow from, this feature are then derived, together with any further features which are required if any of these features are to form part of a world comprehensible to the protagonist. These features will in turn lead to further features, so continuing the construction of the model world. A distinction can be maintained throughout between how the world appears to the protagonist on the inside and how it appears to us on the outside. On the inside it is at an extremely primitive level but this is possible since, from the outside, it is being constructed in the context of our present scheme.

The device of using model worlds enables us, who construct them, to think on both sides of the limit of comprehensibility. It is possible for us, for example, to consider some essential feature as if it were not essential, and so discover it to be essential. It is also possible for us to study some feature which is in fact impossible, and so discover it to be so. If all study of the essential features of any comprehensible world had to be by examining or modifying the features of our present world, then features which were impossible could never be studied and found to be impossible. However, if we study a model world set in the context of our own world, then it is possible to study such features and find that they are impossible. In this way the device of building a model world enables us to think on both sides of the limit of comprehensibility.

The model world constructed in the course of the following inquiry will be called the general model world. It is useful to call it a model world since this serves as a reminder of its fundamental starting-point, of the fact that it is constructed, and of the difference in point of view between the protagonist on the inside of it and we who study the protagonist on the outside of it. However, it is important to remember that terms like 'construction' and 'model world' are analogical, since what happens in the so-called construction of the general model world is that the necessity of certain features is derived from the necessity of other features, which is not the same thing as laying one solid part on top of another solid part, as happens in the construction not only of normal ships and houses, but also of model ships and houses. It is also the case that the features themselves, particularly those derived in the earlier stages of the inquiry, tend to be general or formal in their nature, relating to the structure of a comprehensible world as a whole rather than to any kind of thing that it should contain. This makes deriving one of these features from another even less like laying one solid thing on top of another.

The construction of this general model world forms the backbone to the following inquiry. In order to achieve it considerable use will be made of particular model worlds which will be introduced as required. In these particular model worlds formal or structural features are given particular content. This helps in examining such features and makes it possible to see what other features they involve. Since formal or structural features are given particular content in these particular model worlds, they are complete in themselves and are therefore model worlds in a much less analogical sense that is the general model world. They possess the same advantages as it; in that it is possible for us to distinguish between how a feature appears to us and how it appears to the protagonist of a particular model world, in that particular model worlds can be exceedingly primitive or simple; and in that we can use them to think on both sides of the limit of comprehensibility. Their nature and use should become quite clear in the course of the inquiry.

§11   'COMPREHENSIBLE' AS 'COMPREHENSIBLE TO US'

Even if the inquiry does start at a very fundamental level, as recommended in §9 and held to be possible in §10, it still seems as if it is only the nature of worlds which are comprehensible to us or to someone like us that can be studied. For even if a split is made between us on the outside of the general model world and the protagonist on the inside, it is still we who have to decide whether or not something would be comprehensible to the protagonist; and it does not seem that we could decide this unless we are able to assume that the protagonist understands in the same way that we ourselves understand, which is to assume that the protagonist's comprehension is like our own. Yet if this is so, it might seem to limit the scope of the inquiry, since it shows that it is not an inquiry into the essential features of any comprehensible world *simpliciter* but, rather, an inquiry into the essential features of any world which is to be comprehensible to someone like ourselves.

Whether or not it does form an objection to the scope of the inquiry, it will be demonstrated in the present section that an inquiry such as the present one can indeed be only into the essential features of a world comprehensible to someone like ourselves, and that this means the essential features of a world which can be thought about and judged in a similar way to the way we think about and judge our own world. It is only if 'comprehensible' is understood as meaning 'comprehensible to us' that it is possible for us who are making the study to distinguish between comprehensible and incomprehensible situations. For unless the means we use to distinguish between comprehensible and incomprehensible situations in the inquiry has a basis in the means that we use to make this distinction in the present world, it can only be merely stipulative and arbitrary. It would be intolerably arbitrary, that is, if some feature were just to be designated as making the difference between comprehensible and incomprehensible situations, and this arbitrariness can only be avoided if we take some feature which we at present use to distinguish between comprehensible and incomprehensible situations in our own world.

Furthermore, it is not the case that just any feature of situations in which we comprehend our present world can be taken as criterial in deciding whether or not the protagonist comprehends his world. For we can only decide whether the protagonist comprehends his world by thinking of how the world would appear to him; and we can only decide this by thinking of how the world would appear to us if we were in his position. Yet this is to decide how we would think about, and judge, the world from his position. So we can only think about the protagonist at all if we can think of him as having, at least in primitive terms, thought and judgement similar to our own thought and judgement. As Kant says: 'if I wish to represent to myself a thinking being, I must put myself in his place, and thus substitute, as it were, my own subject for the object I am seeking to consider' (CPR, A353).

If the inquiry is to be possible at all, therefore, we must take the protagonist as comprehending his world in a similar way to the way we comprehend our world, and this means that we must take him to be thinking about or judging his world. It might seem that this was too strong and that some other features of our present situation apart from properties of thought or judgement could be used as criteria for deciding whether someone or something comprehended its world or not. Thus is might be suggested that if someone survived in a world, or if he built mechanical objects, or if he had a developed social life, then he comprehends that world. Examples show, however, that it is not possible to take such alternative features as being criteria for comprehensibility. A primitive unicellular organism immersed in a world full of nourishing fluid would survive in it, but it could hardly be said that such an organism comprehends its world. Again, building complex objects may be instinctive, and not evince comprehension of a world; for spiders build complex objects, and can hardly be said to comprehend the world. Ants have a highly developed social life. The only certain test, the only thing which can be taken as a criterion, when deciding whether or not the protagonist understands his world, is the structure or nature of the protagonist's thought and judgement. This is both what we are inevitably drawn into studying (as the Kant quotation remarks) if we are studying whether someone understands his world, and is also the only area in which we can find non-arbitrary criteria worthy of extended study.

It might still be thought, however, that this was too strong a test and that someone who engaged in a complex pattern of activity similar to complex activities engaged in by people in the present world would evince comprehension of his world. Consider, however, the analogous claim that a group (a tribe of people, for example) can clearly be said to use and understand mathematics if they use things that look like slide-rules in the course of building complex objects like cars or bridges. Here we could never be justified in saying that they understood and used mathematics unless we could translate into our mathematics, and so understand, the connections between the slide-rules and the bridge or car. It is just possible, that is, that the tribe just happened to get the right dimensions for their cars or bridges without calculating them, in the same way that the spider just happens to get the right dimensions for parts of his web. This might be thought improbable, but then it is improbable that the tribe were using something which looked exactly like our slide-rules at all (and we could not tell, of course, of something that looked different that it was being used as a slide-rule unless we could translate the rules by which they were using it).

In general, logically possible cases only show possibilities and impossibilities and are of no help in the evaluation of probability. This particular case of the cars and the slide-rules does not show that the tribe possesses a deviant mathematics with quite different rules not understandable by us but, rather, shows that the ability to build cars is only contingently connected with the ability to use and understand mathematics. It would be good evidence, that is, in an actual case, that a tribe could understand and use mathematics, but it would only be good evidence for this because it is also good evidence for thinking that, if only we kept looking long enough, we would be able to discover the connections between the use of the slide-rules and the construction of the car. It would not be evidence that, if no such connections could be found, the tribe was nevertheless able to understand and use mathematics. In this case of mathematical understanding, therefore, we can only be justified in ascribing it to people who understand mathematically in basically the same way as we do; people for whom it is possible to translate the rules of their procedure into something we recognize as mathematics; people in whose place it is possible for us to put ourselves.

It seems that the situation for the study of comprehension in general is the same as that for the study of mathematical comprehension. The only way that such a study can possibly be made is if we distinguish between comprehension and incomprehension by taking comprehension as being comprehension in the same way that we at present comprehend; and that we can only do this if we are able to think of ourselves as being in the situation of the person being studied, and examining whether the structure of his thought or judgement is similar to that of our thought and judgement. If some other feature of our present world, apart from the structure of thought and judgement were to be taken, it would not be possible to think of ourselves as being in the protagonist's position, and so not be possible to have an inquiry such as the present one.

It is necessary, then, if there is going to be an inquiry at all, that it should be into the essential features of a world that can be comprehended in a way similar to the way we comprehend at present. This means that unless the protagonist can be taken as exhibiting a pattern of thought and judgement which is, at least in very primitive terms, similar to the pattern of our own thought and judgement, then the inquiry can not take place. This, of course, does not justify us assuming that the protagonist does exhibit such a structure, for perhaps the inquiry is not worth undertaking, or impossible. Just because these are necessary conditions for undertaking the inquiry, that is, is not sufficient reason for assuming that they apply, for they could equally well be taken as sufficient reason for holding that the price of the inquiry is too high for it to be worth while. In the next section, however, it will be shown that these assumptions which have to be made if the inquiry is to take place are assumptions which are perfectly justifiable. It will be shown that these assumptions form no limitation or objection to the inquiry, and that, on the contrary, indicating them shows the proper place from which construction of the model world should begin.

§12   THE PROTAGONIST AS JUDGER OF HIS WORLD

In the last section it was argued that an inquiry into the essential conditions of any world being a comprehensible one was not possible unless 'comprehension' was taken as meaning 'comprehension in the same way as we comprehend', and that this involved assuming both that the protagonist thought about and judged his world and also that this judgement was (at least in primitive terms) similar in form to our judgement. It seemed that this apparent limitation on the inquiry might spoil its scope and power, rendering its conclusions too parochial to be interesting. If we wish to study comprehensibility as such, it may seem disappointing to be limited to ourselves; for we may well regard the limitations on our present form of thought and judgement as being in principle avoidable and think that God, for example, does better.

If, however, the conclusions of Chapter One are remembered, then this restriction to ourselves and our own form of thought and judgement no longer seems to be a limitation on the inquiry. For the chief reason why it was held to be desirable to have an inquiry into the essential features of any comprehensible world was because it emerged in Chapter One that there were certain assumptions that someone who was studying the world with the use of pure reason alone would be justified in making. Among these was that the world was a comprehensible one; for it was held (in §5) that any world in which we could conceivably have any interest was one that we could comprehend. Since we could have no interest in a situation for which this condition did not apply, we are justified in assuming *a priori* that it does apply, and so may study what the world is like with the use of pure reason alone by working out the essential conditions of the world being a comprehensible one. It will be noticed that no further limitation will be placed on such an inquiry if 'comprehensible' is understood as meaning 'comprehensible in the same way as we comprehend'. For, again, we could have no interest in a situation which was not comprehensible to us, or to someone like us. So when the essential conditions of a world being comprehensible are considered, this may equally well be understood as the essential conditions of a world being comprehensible to someone like us. For although this appears to be a limitation, it allows an inquiry to take place which serves the purposes of any such inquiry as well as the original stipulation would.

So the necessary conditions on the inquiry which emerged in the last section are perfectly justifiable and form no limitation on it once it is remembered why the inquiry as a whole is being undertaken. The corollary of the condition which emerged in the last section, that we had to think of the protagonist as judging his world if we were going to be able to study whether he comprehended it or not, is that we cannot be interested in any situation in which someone or something comprehends his world unless it is possible for us to be in his situation and so to comprehend his world. Since this involves thought and judgement, it is perfectly proper for us to assume from the *a priori* position that the world is such that it can be thought about and judged. In the general model world, therefore, it is perfectly proper to assume that the protagonist thinks about, and judges, his world. Although it seems at first to be a restriction to be limited to the study of our kind of comprehension, and so to the study of our form of thought and judgement, it turns out that it is not a restriction in that we are justified in assuming that any world in which we could be interested must be subject to just this kind of comprehension. We come into the equation in two ways and these two ways cancel out. Since it is we who make the study, we are limited to our kind of comprehension. But since we make the study to see what must be the case in any world, we can comprehend, this forms no effective limitation.

Remembering why the inquiry is being undertaken not only shows that these apparent limitations are not real limitations, but also shows where the inquiry should begin. The whole point, or trick, involved in these transcendental arguments, as explained in §7, was to take attention away from the object of apprehension and apply it to the medium by which it was apprehended. By study of the medium, the idea is to discover the nature of any objects that can be apprehended by use of this medium. The medium studied in the present inquiry is thought or judgement, and so it is hoped that by study of the essential nature of thought or judgement, the essential nature of objects which can be thought about or judged will be discovered. This medium is selected because it is a medium which must apply to any world in which we could possibly be interested; we can only be interested, that is, in worlds which can be apprehended by use of this medium. Since the medium is thought or judgement it is also a medium the study of which is possible by pure reason alone: it seems appropriate that thought should be able to untangle the preconditions or essential consequences of thought in the way that it could not of another medium.

This being the case, the fundamental features with which construction of the model world will begin will obviously be the absolutely central properties of all thought or judgement. The hope in constructing the model world is to be able to move from such central or obvious properties of thought and judgement to other less obvious properties. All the time this study of the medium circumscribes the nature of any world to which the medium can be applied; as features are derived in construction of the general model world, so is a picture built up of any world which can be judged or described. By studying the medium, the nature of any object to which the medium can be applied becomes apparent. The inquiry starts with the general properties of thought and judgement and ends with the particular properties of any world that can be thought about or judged.

The features with which the inquiry begins, therefore, are the very general, central, and basic properties of thought and judgement. Some of these will be assumed in order to begin construction of the general model world. To do this is, in the light of the arguments of the last section, to take thought and judgement in the way that we think and judge (or could understand to be thought and judgement). As has been shown in this section, however, this is a harmless limitation. It means that the central properties of thought from which the inquiry begins will be properties of our own thought; but since this is the only kind of thought that we could be interested in, this contains no real restriction.

It was argued in §§9 and 10 that the inquiry must start from a fundamental starting-point and not just start with our present situation. Thus it was argued that the essential features of any comprehensible world should be discovered by construction rather than being uncovered by reduction from the present situation. It has now been argued in §11, and justified in this section, that the inquiry can only proceed if we understand by 'comprehension' comprehension in the same way that we at present comprehend. It might seem that these positions were in conflict, and that these later arguments eliminate the possibility of using the fundamental starting-point argued for in the earlier sections. This, however, is not the case. All that the last two sections have shown is the position from which the inquiry must begin. It has not been shown that this position is not a fundamental position, but that the features assumed in the starting position, which can be as fundamental as we desire, are features involving thought and judgement, and involving our present kind of thought and judgement. These last sections do not show that we cannot start with fundamental features and construct a model world. All they show is the nature of the fundamental features with which we must begin such a construction; that such fundamental features are not just features of thought or judgement as such, but also features of our kind of thought or judgement.

§13 PREMISSES AND LAYERS OF CERTAINTY

It has been seen that the inquiry as a whole can be taken as the construction of a model world, to be called the general model world. In this construction, which is more a matter of deducing certain features from others than anything more directly like building, the essential features which must be possessed by any comprehensible world are discovered. This is done by starting with certain essential features, and by seeing which other ones these presuppose or imply, and also by seeing which other features must be present if these features are going to form part of a world comprehensible to its protagonist. Since it is comprehension that is being considered, the initial features will relate to the nature of the protagonist's comprehension. It has been seen that this involves them relating to the nature of the protagonist's thought and judgement, and that such thought and judgement must be taken as being similar to our own. So the initial features which must be assumed, or premised, in order to get the inquiry started, will be particular properties of the protagonist's thought or judgement.

The inquiry can only start with premising the existence of some particular features in the general model world; for unless some features are premised at the outset, it is impossible to derive other features from them. On the other hand, even though it starts with premises, it is hoped that these premises should be as certain as possible. Ideally they will be premises which it is as justifiable to assume from the *a priori* point of view as the original assumption that the world was such that it could be thought about and judged. They should, therefore, relate to the very basic properties of thought as such. Only those features which seem to be absolutely essential if there can be judgement of a world at all should be adopted as premises. So in searching for features with which to begin the inquiry, we want to search for features without which thought or judgement would be impossible, or at least without which we cannot conceive how there could be thought or judgement.

Ultimately, of course, the basis on which the premisses rest can only be agreement. In that they are premisses, they can only be argued for informally, and can not be demonstrated conclusively. Anyone who does not agree with them will not be bound by the inquiry which follows from them. However, this having been said, there are certain properties which we can be fairly certain are absolutely essential if there is going to be thought and judgement about a world, and on which we may expect general agreement. There are other features which seem to be less necessary, or about which we are less certain whether they are necessary or not. On these we can expect less agreement, and so they would form less desirable premisses. On the other hand, they may be needed in the course of the argument.

In the circumstances the best tactic seems to be the following. Construction of the general model world should begin with the assumption of just one premiss. This should be about some feature for which it is absolutely certain that it will be a feature of any comprehensible world, and so be a premiss about which we can expect universal agreement. The consequences of this first premiss will then be derived as far as possible. When no more can be made of it, a second premiss can be added which is slightly less necessary, or about which we are slightly less certain whether it is necessary or not. The hope is that nearly everyone will also agree to this and so be bound by the following argument in which the consequences of these first two premisses are investigated. The process can then be repeated. In this way the general model world will fall into layers of necessity or certainty. Each layer is introduced by a new premiss. Each layer depends upon the layer before it, but it is slightly less certain in each succeeding layer whether the features which are derived in it are really features of any comprehensible world or not. The argument depends on agreement about the premisses, and at a certain stage someone may find that he disagrees about a premiss, and so finds that he is not bound by the subsequent argument. By introducing the premisses in succession, each dictating the degree of certainty or apparent necessity of a layer of the general model world, such disagreement is avoided for as long as possible, or may indeed never appear at all.

Another reason why it is important to order the degrees of certainty of the various layers of the general model world in this way is that this is the best way of achieving one of the purposes of the inquiry. It will be remembered that in §8 it was argued both that this inquiry could be used to answer certain notorious sceptical arguments and that this was important in that such sceptical arguments could not merely be brushed aside as offending against common sense. Now if the inquiry is to form an answer to scepticism, then its starting-points must be absolutely certain. The more certain the starting-points are, the more effective the argument will be in demolishing sceptical positions. So, again, it is better to start with absolutely certain premises and to introduce less certain ones later if they should become required. In this way, while the later stages of the argument may only provide some kind of answer to the sceptical positions examined in them, the earlier stages will be able to demolish other sceptical positions completely. So, again, introduction of the premises in succession means that the maximum advantage can be gained from them.

The task of the inquiry, however, is not just to defeat notorious sceptical arguments. It also aims to give some insight into the structure of any comprehensible world, and so of our present world, by showing which parts of it are essentially connected with others, and which parts are not so closely related to others as might be assumed. This task will also be achieved by constructing the general model world in layers. By sorting out the layers, or levels, of the general model world, it will be found which features are intimately related with which others; and which are so un-related that they only appear in a different layer of the general model world. The construction of the general model world in levels will also therefore give insight into the relations between the features themselves.

This second task of giving insight into the relations of the features themselves seems at first sight to be ontological, or metaphysical; and so does not seem to be related at all to the anti-sceptical task, which is epistemological. However, when it is shown that certain features are equally essential; when it is shown that certain features are interconnected so that some are necessary for others; when it is shown that certain features are not so closely connected as might be assumed, it is epistemological necessity, closeness, or lack of connection that is being demonstrated. Features shown to be necessary, that is, are features which are necessary in any comprehensible world. Features shown to be closely related are features which must be so related in any comprehensible world. When it is shown that features are not so closely related as might be assumed, what is shown is that it is not necessary for comprehension of a world that they be so related. Although, therefore, the inquiry aims to give insight into the relations or non-relations between certain features as well as answering sceptical arguments, this second task is also an epistemological one, and also one performed naturally by constructing the general model world. For the kinds of relation which it is desired to discover are epistemological relations.

The general model world, that is, expresses the relations between certain features, showing which depend upon which and which are independent. This looks at first sight like a purely metaphysical, or ontological, project. It is also one which gives insight into the nature of our present world, since the features of our own present world satisfy the relations expressed in the general model world. The relations involved, however, are all epistemological. The task of the inquiry, which is the task of all transcendental arguments, is to find the necessary conditions for there to be thought about, or judgement of, a world. This is an epistemological task. The resulting necessary conditions show which features and relations are epistemologically necessary. Discovering such necessary conditions will both enable us to answer certain notorious sceptical arguments and also enable us to gain insight into the relations between features in a world such as our own. We discover which things must be the case, not for general logical or metaphysical reasons, but because they must be the case if we are to comprehend the world. These are the kind of necessities that the inquiry investigates; yet investigating them does not merely exorcise sceptical demons but also gives us some real insight into the nature of the world itself. It shows us in a new way the function and importance of certain elements of our present world.

In the inquiry which follows, then, the fundamental or essential features of any comprehensible world will be discovered by constructing a model world comprehensible to its protagonist and called the general model world. Construction will be started by means of a first premiss which assumes that this world contains some feature which seems to be an absolutely essential feature of any comprehensible world. Since the idea is to move from the nature of the medium to the nature of the world, this first feature will be some very central property of thought or judgement. From this first feature others will be derived until no more can be derived. Then a new premiss will be used to introduce another feature. Use of this premiss will move the inquiry to a lesser level of certainty or necessity; the model world can be thought of as moving to another layer, a layer which presupposes all the features derived in its inmost, most certain layer, but a layer in which further features can be derived which depend upon this new premiss as well. The process will then be repeated, gradually reducing the certainty of the premisses and gradually adding layers to the model world which contain successively less certain or central features. Construction of the general model world in this manner will enable us both to demonstrate which features are essential, and so to show the content of the present world, and also to demonstrate how essential the relations between some of these particular features are, and so give insight into the relative importance of elements of our present world.

CHAPTER THREE

Connection of Judgements

§14 INTRODUCTION AND INFORMAL ARGUMENT

IN the last chapter it was seen that the inquiry as a whole should take the form of the construction of a model world to be called the general model world. This construction proceeds by assuming some very central and essential feature of any comprehensible world, and then deriving its consequences and preconditions. This central feature will be a feature of any world which can be thought about or judged, and so will reflect an essential property of thought or judgement. To find it we must reflect upon the nature of our own thought and judgement and select some feature of it which seems absolutely essential. When we have done this we can assume by means of the first premiss of the inquiry that this feature is part of the general model world, and so begin its construction. As a premiss, it ultimately depends upon assumption and agreement, and the first premiss will be introduced and used as an unsupported premiss in the next section. Before it is formally introduced, however, it is worth considering in a more informal way the nature of our thought and judgement in order to give as much support as possible to the first premiss; and in order to be as certain as possible that it really is essential.

If we look in this informal way at the nature of our judgements, it seems possible to claim that in any judgement about the world there is a referential and a descriptive element. It seems, that is, that a distinction can be drawn between what a judgement is about and what this judgement says about it. If this is so, then the problem of what is essential if there is to be judgement of a world can be broken down into two questions: whether anything is essential if there is to be reference to particular parts of a world, and whether anything is essential if these parts are to be described. If anything seems quite clearly to be essential for either activity, then it seems safe to adopt this feature as the first premiss of the inquiry, declaring that this feature is essential in any world we could comprehend.

It is tempting to think that such a feature can be produced by means of an answer to the first question, the question of whether anything is essential if there is to be reference to particular parts of a world. It is in this area that Strawson argues with effect in the first chapter of *Individuals*. Now if Strawson is right in his long battle with Quine during the Fifties about the eliminability of singular terms, then some token-reflexive or context-dependent element is essential in all judgement if reference is to be guaranteed (if it is to be certain that the reference is to one particular object rather than to another exactly similar one). This enables Strawson to argue that reference will only be guaranteed if there is a single ordering system which connects everything referred to to the present situation of the speaker, and so enables him to argue for the fundamental role played by bodies linked in a single spatio-temporal system. It seems, therefore, that a rich harvest of conclusions will follow if some feature can be isolated which is essential if uniqueness of reference is to be guaranteed, such as that everything judged has to be connected by a unique route with the judger's own position.

The features which Strawson uses to start his argument, however, could not be adopted as the features with which to start the present inquiry. For it does not seem essential for there to be reference at all that it must be possible for reference to be guaranteed. Suppose, that is, that Strawson's point against Quine is granted and it is recognized that it is always logically possible that a reference which relies only on description (for example, 'the red biro with spots') should be ambiguous. This does not imply that it would be impossible for there to be reference at all if only such descriptions could be used. They would, for example, be quite adequate if there were not in fact any massive duplications in the world so that they were not in fact ambiguous. If only pure descriptions could be used to make reference, some references would in fact fail, and no reference could be logically guaranteed not to fail. This does not, however, mean that reference would be impossible. It is not obvious, that is, and at the very least needs further argument, that in order for there to be reference at all, it has to be possible to guarantee uniqueness of reference. A feature which guarantees uniqueness of reference, therefore, is not a sufficiently certain basis to be adopted for the present inquiry. This would not necessarily worry Strawson who is concerned with what he calls 'descriptive metaphysics' and so is concerned with isolating and describing features nearer the surface of our present system. It means, however, that Strawson's starting-point cannot be used in the present inquiry, in which an extremely fundamental and obviously essential feature of our judgement of any world is to be adopted as the first premiss.

If it does not seem that such an essential feature can be isolated by examining what is required in any world in which there is to be reference to parts of that world, then it must be seen whether such a feature can be isolated by seeing whether anything is required in any world in which such parts can be described. In any case, as analysed by both Quine and Strawson, description is presupposed by reference. On this ground alone, therefore, it would seem more natural to look for an essential condition for the description of any world when looking for an essential feature of all judgement. This is to turn to the second of the two questions into which the original problem was split, the question of whether anything is essential if the parts of a world are to be described.

Let us take a simple particular model world in order to examine this question more closely, and to help in producing an informal argument for an answer to it (which is all that this section claims to provide). This world can be designed to place the maximum emphasis on description and the minimum emphasis on reference. So suppose that it just consists of a succession of single total states, $v, w, x, y \ldots$ Inside it is the protagonist who judges it. The question is what is essential if these judgements are to be taken as descriptions of his world. Since reference is taken to be at a minimum, the protagonist can be taken to be referring to the particular state with which he is confronted at any one time. Attention, that is, can be concentrated on the descriptive elements of the judgements. Now suppose the protagonist judges 'a', 'b', 'c', 'd' . . . The question is, to repeat, what is essential if these judgements are going to be taken as descriptive of the situation (or, it could be said, are going to be judgements at all).

Now it seems obvious that, to put it crudely, these can only be taken to be judgements of the situation if there is some connection between the particular judgements and the particular states of the world. The first judgement, 'a', that is, can only be thought of as being a judgement of the first state of the world, v, if there is something more to connect it with v than there is with w or x. Similarly with 'b' and w and with 'c' and x. There must, that is, be something like the choice or selection of judgements as being appropriate to the situation. This can be seen if the above series of judgements is compared with a case in which the protagonist, for example, was confronted with a similar series of states of the world and just judged 'h', 'h', 'h', 'h' . . . In this latter case he could not be taken to be judging his world, since he could not be taken to be referring to each present state of his world and to be describing it.

Even granted that the protagonist has to display something akin to choice if he is to be taken to be describing his world, the question still remains of which way the protagonist needs to choose his judgements in order to count as describing his world. Granted, that is, that 'a' in the first situation described is connected with v in a way that it is not with w, the question still remains of what the nature of this connection is. It could be said that the protagonist must choose the judgements which apply to the world, and that the connection between the judgements that it is appropriate for him to choose and the states of the world is that the judgements describe the states, or that the judgements are the true ones. Such further explanation, however, is not particularly helpful since it is just what makes judgements descriptive of states of affairs that is in question.

One conclusion does seem to emerge, however, out of this informal argument and the description of this particular model world. This is that if a protagonist is taken to comprehend his world, he must be able to select between the judgements that he could make, and select those that apply to the world. This seems a fundamental feature which must be present if a protagonist is to be taken to be judging or comprehending a world at all, and so one which it is safe to assume as basic. It will accordingly form the basis of the first premiss of the inquiry.

It seems to emerge from study of this particular model world, that is, that a protagonist cannot be taken to comprehend his world if he just offers judgements at random. On the contrary, he must be taken as giving some weight to the quality of truth-aimedness that exists in judgements; he must be taken as selecting some judgements in preference to others because these judgements are true of the world, are about the world. So it seems that it is an essential condition for comprehension of any world that it must be possible in that world to distinguish between the judgements which apply to the world and the judgements which do not apply to the world. This is the condition which will be adopted in a more extended form as the first premiss. It seems acceptable enough on its own terms but if any extra support for it is felt to be required, this should be provided by the informal arguments of this section.

§15 THE FIRST PREMISS

In the last section it was indicated that a fundamental feature of any comprehensible world was that the protagonist (of that world) should be able to make some distinction between those judgements that he could make which would be true (or apply to the world), and those judgements that he could make which would be false (would not apply to the world). This will form part of the first premiss of the inquiry. In its full form this premiss will be that, in any comprehensible world, there must be reasons available to the protagonist enabling him to distinguish between those judgements of his which are true and those judgements of his which are false. This is obviously a stronger claim than the feature that was argued for informally in the last section. However, it is fairly easy to show that it is both essential in any comprehensible world and also extremely fundamental. The feature argued for informally in the last section was that the protagonist must be able to distinguish between true and false judgements. Now it is obvious that the distinction must be made by means of something apart from the judgements themselves. For judgements do not carry their truth-values on their face. Something apart from the immediate judgements being distinguished must therefore be available to the protagonist if he is to be able to make the distinction. That is, reasons must be available to the protagonist enabling him to distinguish between those judgements of his which are true and those judgements of his which are false.

If the premiss in its extended form did not apply, then any member of a series of judgements made by the protagonist would appear to him to have the same standing, even though the series might contain mutually incompatible, or mutually contradictory, judgements. For example, the judgement '*a*' and the judgement '*not-a*' would have exactly the same standing at the same time for the protagonist unless there were reasons available to him which supported one of them rather than the other. In this case, '*a*' and '*not-a*', being mutually contradictory, cannot both be true. Yet if something else apart from the judgements themselves is not available to the protagonist, then he can have no way of distinguishing between them. So unless reasons are available to him, enabling him to distinguish between his true and his false judgements, mutually contradictory judgements such as '*a*' and '*not-a*' would have the same standing for him. Or to put it another way, if there were no reasons available to him enabling him to select which of his judgements applied to the world, then at any time he judged '*a*', he might as well have judged '*not-a*'. Yet a protagonist for which both '*a*' and '*not-a*' had exactly the same standing would not be a protagonist who was able to distinguish between his true and his false judgements, and would not be a protagonist who comprehended his world.

It seems to be a fundamental feature of our comprehension of a world, that is, that when we have no reason to assert that A, rather than asserting that not-A, then there is no point making either assertion if we wish to assert something about the world. For, if no reasons are available to support either judgement, one of them might as well be asserted as the other. However, both of them cannot be asserted at the same time (since they are mutually contradictory) and so, until some reasons are available which support one of them rather than the other, there is no point in asserting either of them. This is why the premiss that emerged at the end of the last section has been extended so that it now becomes the assumption that reasons must be available to the protagonist, enabling him to distinguish between those judgements of his which are true (or are taken by him to be true), and those judgements of his which are false (or are taken by him to be false). This seems to be an obvious and fundamental assumption whose alternative seems to be wildly implausible; unless this condition is met it does not seem that a world could be a comprehensible one.

This premiss is the one adopted in this inquiry since it seems extremely obvious and extremely fundamental. It arises naturally out of the idea of judgement, and it has been seen that we must think of any comprehension like our own, any comprehension that we could think ourselves on the inside of, as one which makes judgements. It seems to seize upon the most central and essential characteristic of judgements, that they can be true or false, that they can be about the world or not about the world. This has been seen to involve selection between possible judgements, and it does not seem that there could be such selection unless there were reasons available to the person making the selection enabling him to distinguish between the judgements which belonged to the one class and the judgements which belonged to the other class. Accordingly, the first premiss of the inquiry is that reasons are available to the protagonist of the general model world (of any comprehensible world) enabling him to distinguish between those judgements of his which are true and those judgements of his which are false.

A corollary of this first premiss is that in any comprehensible world, incompatible judgements depend upon differences in the reasons available for supporting these judgements. If, that is, the protagonist's judgements are not completely idle, or not really judgements at all, then there must be differences in the reasons available to him between the time or situation in which he judges that a and the time or situation in which he judges that $not\text{-}a$. It might seem more convenient to assume this corollary as the first premiss, since it makes no overt mention of the difficult notions of truth or falsehood. However, if it were to be adopted as a premiss, its validity would depend upon a tacit assumption of the present first premiss. This is because the point of asserting that there must be differences in the reasons available between times or situations in which the two members of an incompatible pair of judgements are made is that one (or both) of such a pair of judgements must be false unless they are made at different times or in different situations, and that reasons will be needed to distinguish which of the two (if either) is true at any one time or situation. So there is no point in adopting this corollary as a rival first premiss.

Returning to the first premiss that has been adopted, it is important to notice that no commitment is implied by it to any temporal order applying between the judgements of the protagonist and his acknowledgement or recognition of the reasons for the truth of these judgements. In the first place, it has not yet been shown that time is a feature of the general model world. However, even if time is a feature of the general model world and so meaning can be given to a temporal order applying between the recognition of reasons and the making of judgements, the first premiss does not assert that the recognition of reasons must precede the making of judgements. On the contrary, the requirements of the first premiss would quite properly be met by a situation in which reasons were acknowledged or recognized after the judgements for which they were reasons had been made. The premiss, that is, asserts that reasons must be available to the protagonist. It does not assert that he need actually use reasons in making judgements, or that he need be aware of the reasons before he makes a judgement.

It is important also to realize that the first premiss would be satisfied by a condition in which the protagonist never made a mistake and always judged correctly. All that is required to fulfil the first premiss is that the protagonist must be able to select among the judgements that he could make at any one time those judgements that he takes to be true. This means that he must take some of the judgements he makes or could make as being true (as applying to the world) and that he must take some of the judgements that he makes or could make as being false (as not applying to the world). This, however, does not imply that all the judgements he actually makes might not be true. The protagonist, therefore, is still permitted by the first premiss to be right the whole time, provided that the judgements he makes are thought of as selected from among the judgements that he could have made, others of which (if he had made them) would have been false. His situation in such a case would be analogous to the situation in which God is in in Leibniz's world; God there knows all the possible monads that he could endow with existence but he always chooses to endow those monads with existence which together compose the best possible world.

It might be thought that, although the case in which the protagonist is always right is perfectly compatible with the first premiss, it could be developed in order to suggest an alternative premiss. For it looks as though someone who is right in every judgement he makes about the world must be said to be able to comprehend it; and yet it seems possible that someone could do this without there being any idea of his selecting between the judgements that he could have made, and so without there having to be any reasons available which enable him to make such a selection. It might be thought, that is, that the case in which the protagonist is always right shows that the availability of reasons is not essential in every comprehensible world, and so shows that the first premiss does not, after all, isolate an essential feature of any comprehensible world. This is obviously a plausible objection and will be considered carefully in §19 by when there will be both further reasons to consider it and also more material available with which to deal with it. In the meantime it is sufficient to realize that the first premiss does not imply that the protagonist need actually make mistakes in judgement; for the first premiss is satisfied if he selects the judgements that he does make from among judgements some of which, if he had made them, would have been mistaken.

§16   HISTORICAL USE OF THE FIRST PREMISS

Leibniz took his philosophy as resting on two premisses or principles, the principle of non-contradiction and the principle of sufficient reason. Of these two it was obviously the latter which gave his philosophy its contingent bite and enabled Leibniz to deduce conclusions about the actual world. In fact, as he states it it appears to be quite simply a cosmological principle (or a scientific principle of great generality) which states how things are in the world. At the beginning of Leibniz's second letter to Clarke, for example, he states it as follows: 'nothing happens without a reason why it should be so rather than otherwise' (*Leibniz-Clarke,* II, 1). This, of course, has been the way that the principle of this name has been understood in succeeding German philosophy from Kant to the early Wittgenstein, where it has been the principle that every event has a cause.

Although Leibniz states and sometimes uses his principle as if it were an ontological one, declaring that there must be a reason why everything in the world happens, sometimes it is given more of an epistemological connotation, declaring that there must be a reason why we take or cause something to happen rather than something else. For example, he relies upon it in his correspondence with Clarke when he wants to argue that there must be a reason why we choose one thing rather than another (IV, 1). It is true that most of the subsequent argument then concerns what God would choose, and so concerns what exists in this world (which God has chosen to create out of all the possible worlds that he could have created). However, in that he is looking at conditions that must apply if God is going to be able to choose at all (such as the identity of indiscernibles, for example (IV, 13)), he is using the principle in a more epistemological way. The principle, that is, is not only used to state what is, or must be, the case, *simpliciter*, but is also used to state what is, or must be, the case if a mind can perform a certain operation on it, such as choosing that it should exist.

Although, therefore, Leibniz uses his principle for God, and so uses it to determine whether God can choose that certain things exist rather than using it to determine whether people such as ourselves can judge that certain things exist, there are obvious similarities between his principle of sufficient reason and the first premiss of the present inquiry. In both cases it is asserted that something must be so if a certain choice is to be made. In the one case the choice is God's choice about which things exist, in the other case it is our choice (or the choice of someone like us) about which judgements about the world are the true ones. In both cases reasons are held to be essential if the choice is to be made.

Much more recently than Leibniz, the first premiss has obvious affinities with the verificationist movement of the Thirties. It is not equivalent to, nor does it imply, the strong form of the verification principle in which the difference between two judgements is held to be just the difference between the reasons that could be given for them (the actual and possible evidence that could be invoked in their support). However, it is closely connected with a weaker form of that principle in which it is held that unless some difference could be produced in the reasons available for two judgements, then they might as well be taken to be the same judgement. It is closely connected with this principle because it depends on the assumption that if a particular difference is held to be a genuine one, then there must be some difference in the reasons available for the two things to be distinguished. This assumption is applied in the premiss to the particular case of the distinction between a judgement being true and its being false.

The attenuated form of verificationism implicit in the first premiss is underlined when it is realized that this premiss is virtually the same as the premiss that Wittgenstein uses in his private language argument. This famous argument has obvious verificationist overtones which are clear, for example, in the following key passage in the argument: 'But in the present case I have no criterion of correctness. One would like to say: whatever is going to seem right to me is right. And that only means that here we can't talk about "right" ' (*Invest.* §258). The principle assumed here is practically the same as the assumption made in the first premiss. It is that unless there are reasons or criteria available to me enabling me to distinguish between judgements which are right (true) and judgements which are not right (false) then we can't talk about right judgements (and so, presumably, can't talk about judgements at all). The first premiss, therefore, is one which Wittgenstein also found natural to assume as a premiss, and it has interesting connections with one that was assumed by Leibniz. This should increase confidence in its obviousness and its certainty.

§17   IMMEDIATE DEDUCTIONS FROM THE
FIRST PREMISS

In §15 it was assumed as the first premiss of the inquiry that reasons must be available to the protagonist of the general model world (that is, of any comprehensible world) enabling him to distinguish between those judgements of his which are true and those judgements of his which are false. This was also put in the form that reasons must be available to the protagonist enabling him to select, among the judgements that he does or could make, those judgements that are true. The time has now come to make deductions from this premiss, and to derive further features of the general model world from this first feature introduced by it. By examining what must be the case in any world which is to contain this feature, we can discover which other features are essential in any comprehensible world. In this way we can construct the inmost, that is the most certain and essential, layer of the general model world.

The first thing which follows from this feature—that reasons must be available to the protagonist enabling him to distinguish between his judgements—is what can loosely be expressed as connection between judgements. (The precise sense of this will be made clear shortly.) This is because the reasons which are available to the protagonist enabling him to distinguish between his judgements will themselves be expressible as further judgements of his. The reasons available to the protagonist, that is, are either actually expressed in further judgements of his, or at least could be expressed in further judgements of his. So the reasons that the first premiss has assumed must be available to the protagonist must themselves be expressible as judgements. (It might be thought that this was doubtful, and that it would be possible for reasons to be available to the protagonist without it being the case that these reasons were expressible as judgements. This objection will be examined and dismissed in §19; in the meantime it will be assumed that it does not hold.) The reasons available to the protagonist, then, will themselves be expressible as further judgements. Yet if these reasons are really going to be available to him, it must be possible for him to use them to distinguish between his true and his false judgements. If he can do this, there must be some way of distinguishing between the judgements which a reason is a reason for and the judgements which it is not a reason for. So, since the reasons are themselves judgements or expressible as judgements, there has to be some kind of connection between judgements; that is, some means by which those judgements which are reasons can be associated with those judgements for which they form reasons. This means that, if reasons are going to be available to the protagonist, it must be possible for the protagonist to connect his judgements together, which means that there must be some kind of connection between judgements.

It is presumed by the first premiss of the inquiry, that is, that reasons are available to the protagonist. Yet these reasons will themselves be expressible as judgements. They will only be available to the protagonist as reasons, therefore, if it is possible to connect them with the judgements that they are reasons for. This means that it must be possible for the protagonist to connect together judgements, and this will only be possible if there is some kind of connection between judgements. Therefore there is some kind of connection between judgements.

The argument here fits exactly into the predicted pattern of argument when it was described in the last chapter how the general model world would be constructed. After assuming by means of the first premiss that it contains a certain feature, other features are derived from this first feature by seeing what its preconditions are. The model world is constructed by arguing back from a presumed essential condition of any comprehensible world to the necessary conditions of this condition, and to the necessary conditions of these conditions. A certain presumed or derived feature is found to be part of it only if some other feature is part of it. Hence it is demonstrated that this other feature must be part of it. In the present case it is found that reasons can be available to the protagonist only if it is possible for him to connect his judgements together, and that he can connect his judgements together only if these judgements are themselves connected. Hence it is demonstrated that there must be some kind of connection between judgements.

This forms a first result, but it is not yet necessarily an interesting or important result. Perhaps it is possible to be more specific about the kind of connection which must be involved. So far as has been shown, it could be an extremely weak form of connection. It seems in any case as if some extremely weak form of connection between judgements is involved in the first premiss that the protagonist selects between his judgements. For if this selection is thought to be conscious, then the protagonist can be represented as judging that certain judgements that he makes (or might make) are (or would be) false. This is to make a connection between two judgements, the judgement being made and the judgement that that judgement is about. So it might be argued that there is some kind of connection even without bothering about what is involved in reasons; yet this is a form of connection that does not look as if it will lead to any interesting conclusions. It remains to be seen whether the connection between judgements that has been seen to follow from reasons being available to the protagonist is stronger and more interesting than this one.

It might be thought that it need not, since it might be thought that reasons could be given by saying that judgements like the judgement in question were always true. Here there is a connection between judgements, since the original judgement is connected with the further judgement that is being put forward as a reason for it, the judgement that judgements of the same kind as the original judgement are always true. Yet the kind of connection between judgements that is involved here does not look any more promising that the connection that was seen to be involved merely in the conscious declaration that certain judgements were true. However, such a way of attempting to give reasons for a particular judgement being true is not successful. For it just returns the problem to the original problem of how distinction is to be made between the true and the false. The question, that is, would arise immediately of how the distinction was to be made between the kinds of judgement that were always true and the kinds of judgement that were always false. If, that is, it is offered as a reason for a particular judgement being true that judgements of that kind were always true, then a further reason would be required as to why judgements like that were always true. Further reasons would still need to be available to the protagonist, enabling him to distinguish between the kinds of judgement that were always true and the kinds of judgement that were always false; the demand for reasons embodied in the premiss, therefore, cannot be staved off just with the assertion that judgements of the same kind as the judgement in question are always true. Reasons cannot be provided for the truth of judgements which are based only on the kind of judgements that the judgements in question are.

Independent reasons, therefore, are necessary for distinguishing between true and false judgements. Such independent reasons can only be provided by judgements which are themselves logically independent of the judgement in question; judgements, that is, which are about something else and are not just judgements about the judgement in question. One obvious way in which the requirement for the existence of such judgements can be satisfied is by taking judgements of the same type as the judgement in question. This can be illustrated by taking another particular model world in which the bare bones of the features discovered to be essential so far are given flesh by being exemplified in a particular way. Suppose that the protagonist of this particular model world is again taken to be judging total states of his world. It is supposed by the first premiss that he can distinguish those judgements which apply to the world. We may take him, then, as being in a world which is successively in states w, x, y . . . and take him to be judging 'w', 'x', 'y' . . . (the judgements that he has selected as applying to the world). Now the present question is what is involved in the requirement that reasons are available to him which enable him to make such selection (enable him to judge 'w', 'x' . . . rather than 'm', 'm' . . . or 'o', 'p' . . . for example). It has been seen that such reasons cannot just be further judgements about such judgements, but must be logically independent judgements. It is now easy to see which judgements could be used for the purpose in this particular model world. They are the other judgements than the particular judgement which it was desired to give reasons for. For example, when the world is in state x, the protagonist of this particular model world must be able to select the judgement 'x' if he is going to be held to have comprehended it. For this, reasons are needed, and these must be independent of the judgement 'x' itself. The natural and obvious ones to use here are the judgements 'w' and 'y'. If, that is, it is possible for the protagonist to connect together his judgements so that 'w' and 'y' form reasons for the truth of 'x', then reasons will be available to him enabling him to distinguish between those judgements of his which are true and those judgements of his which are false.

This particular model world shows clearly the kind of connection between judgements that is required by the first premiss. For if reasons are to be available to the protagonist

enabling him to distinguish between true and false judgements, then there must be some kind of connection between
these judgements, even though the judgements are logically
independent of each other. A comprehensible world, therefore,
must be such that it is possible to connect together judgements about it in such a way that the truth of some of these
logically independent judgements is connected with the truth
of others of them. How this could operate in a particular
situation is illustrated by the particular model world just
described, in which the truth of any judgement is connected
with judgements of the same level or kind. Here the judgements are logically independent of each other since they are
all simple judgements made at different times about the total
state of the world at that time. Yet if reasons are to be available for the truth or falsity of one of them (and so enable the
protagonist to distinguish between his true judgements and
his false ones), then the truth of this one must be connected
with the truth of the logically independent other judgements.
So, in the case described above, the truth of 'w' and the truth
of 'y' are taken to be reasons for the truth of 'x'; that the
protagonist also judges 'w' and 'y' gives him reason to distinguish 'x' as true.

In the particular case described above, the protagonist of
a particular model world uses the connection between logically independent judgements in order to isolate one of his
judgements as true. It is clear that, in an exactly similar way,
he could isolate another of his judgements as false. For if the
connection between 'x' and 'w' and 'y' provides reason for the
truth of 'x', then it will provide reason for the falsity of any
other judgement that might have been judged at that time.
In the case, above, that is, if the protagonist had misjudged
the total states of his world as 'w', 'p', 'y', then the connection
between the truth of 'w' and 'y' with the truth of 'x' would
enable him to isolate 'p' as false in exactly the same way as
they enable him to isolate 'x' as true.

The connection between judgements required by the first
premiss can also be illustrated by an example taken from our
own present world. Suppose that someone is remembering
what he did the day before. He seems to have separate
memories of seeing Big Ben reading 11 o'clock; seeing the
cenotaph when his watch read 11.05; passing the horse guards;

seeing the Arc de Triomphe in the distance; and standing under Nelson's Column when it was 11.15 on his watch. As long as there is no means of connecting these isolated memories together, then there is no way of deciding which of them are true and which false. However, the manner in which things move round in our present world provides a means for connecting such memories together. By this means the memories can be connected into a coherent story, once the apparent memory about Paris is omitted. So the apparent memories about Whitehall are reasons for each other's truth, and are reasons for the falsity of the apparent memory about the Arc de Triomphe. Since we can connect such memories together, we can provide reasons for the truth or falsity of particular apparent memories.

Once the principle of connection between judgements is established, the need for reasons, and so for further connections, becomes increasingly widespread. For, once there are connections between judgements, then there are also incompatibilities between judgements. A corollary of the first premiss mentioned in §15 is that incompatibilities between judgements imply that there are differences in the reasons available for each member of the incompatible pair. So once there are connections, and consequently incompatibilities, the need for reasons increases. The principle of connection between independent judgements, therefore, not only solves the problem of how reasons are to be given for judgements but also creates a need for a solution to the problem by producing incompatibilities which need to be resolved. This can be seen in terms of the example just given from our present world. For, although the way things move around in our world provides a means of producing reasons for the truth of particular apparent memories, it also provides the need for such reasons. Once such a connection between apparent memories is assumed, that is, then there will be a worrying incompatibility between the apparent memory of Big Ben and the apparent memory of the Arc de Triomphe; a worrying incompatibility which the connection can also be used to resolve. However, if such a connection is not assumed, then there is not such an obvious need to find reasons for the truth of the individual apparent memories since there will then be no such worrying incompatibilities needing elimination.

Once the principle of the connection between independent judgements is established, therefore, occasions for its use will ramify and so the principle will become increasingly well secured. This is not, however, to suggest that the principle only solves a problem which it itself creates. For the principle is needed if there is any incompatibilities between possible judgements. The incompatibilities it itself creates might be called *a posteriori* ones: the world is found to be such that particular judgements are held to be incompatible, although there is nothing incompatible about them *a priori* (they do not, for example, contradict each other). However, there are also obviously *a priori* incompatibilities between the judgements that someone could make at a certain time, for example between the judgements '*A*' and '*not-A*'. The existence of these is sufficient to lead to the demand for reasons which will separate which one is appropriate, and so to the principle of the connection of independent judgements. The principle, therefore, is required quite apart from the problems which it creates itself, and which it can be used to solve.

An immediate deduction from the first premiss, therefore, is that in any comprehensible world it must be possible to connect together logically independent judgements. This is a feature of the basic, or inmost, level of the general model world, being one that is derived directly from the first premiss. It will be remembered that it was just such a feature which was used as an example in §6 when a thumbnail sketch was given of how Kant could be taken to have replied to Hume. For if it has been discovered that it is essential in any comprehensible world that logically independent judgements should be connected together, then, by application of the existential premiss that our own world is a comprehensible one, our own world has been found to be one in which judgements are connected together. Although, that is, there is no logical connection between synthetic, contingent judgements (and Hume is perfectly right about this), we could not comprehend a world in which there was not a non-logical connection between some of the judgements between which there was not such a logical connection. A world would not be a world for us, a world that we could think ourselves as being on the inside of, unless we could connect together such judgements. For if we could not, then we would not be able to use the truth or falsity of some of the judgements as reasons for the truth or falsity of other of the judgements, and so would not be able to distinguish between judgements being true or being false. We must, therefore, be able to make non-logical connections between judgements which are logically indepen-dent of one another.

§18   LAWS

In the last section it was shown that it was a feature of the general model world that the protagonist must be able to connect together judgements which are logically independent of one another. It must now be considered whether there are any necessary conditions which must be satisfied by any world which is to contain this feature. If there are, then, in exactly the same way as this feature was itself derived, these features will have been derived as still further features of the general model world at this, its inmost, level.

So far it is only some kind of connection between logically independent judgements that has been derived, and nothing has been discovered about any particular form which this connection must take. In a particular case of connection, as in the particular model world described in the last section, the protagonist is just taken as being able to assume that the world is such that any particular judgement he is interested in is connected in truth-value with certain other judgements. He isolates 'x', for example, as true because he also judges 'w' and 'y' and because the truth of 'x' is connected with the truth of 'w' and 'y'. So if the protagonist isolates 'x' as true, he can do so only because he relies, implicitly or explicitly, on the principle that 'if "w" and "y" are true, then so is "x" '. Yet this principle, which just connects the particular judge-ment in question with two other particular judgements does not seem able to do the job that is required of it. This can be seen if it is asked by what right the protagonist uses just this principle, or how he could know that the principle itself was true rather than false. For it is obvious that it would not be possible to give any independent support for such a principle: since it is about one particular occasion and nothing else, its support must come only from that occasion. The only thing, that is, which can be used to support the principle 'if "w" and "y" are true, then so is "x" ', is the truth of 'w', 'x', and 'y'.

Yet it is just the truth of (one of) 'w', 'x', and 'y' that is in question and that the principle is meant to decide.

The point is not just that there is a circle in justification so that two things are taken to be supporting each other. It is a different, and more serious, point. This is that the only occasion on which the support provided by something is needed is precisely the occasion on which it is impossible to see if it can give any support. The principle, that is, will only be required on the occasion when there is some doubt about one of the particular judgements that it connects; but if there is doubt about one of the particular judgements it connects, that is precisely the occasion on which it is impossible to produce any support whatsoever for the principle itself.

It is obvious what this particular principle lacks, and what therefore needs to be supplied if it is going to be possible to use the connection of judgements as a means for distinguishing between those judgements which are true and those judgements which are false. This is some generality of application in the principles of connection that are used, so that they themselves can be supported in some cases and then used to distinguish between the true and false judgements in other, more doubtful, cases. If, that is, the principles being used do not only apply to the particular case in question but also apply to many other cases, then it will be possible to rely on them in isolating the true or the false judgements in this particular case. For the support they themselves have will not then depend only on the particular case being examined. Such general principles can be used to decide doubtful cases and if they themselves become doubtful can be supported in other cases; whereas with the kind of particular principle illustrated above there is nothing that can be done outside the case in which it is applied which can give it any support whatsoever (and nothing, of course, can be done to give it support in the case in which it is applied unless it is redundant).

A further requirement of the general model world at this first level, then, is that the principles expressing the connection of judgements should be general in form, and should each apply to many particular cases of connection. This would also seem to be essential if the use of principles of connection is to be practicable. For if there are as many different principles of connection as there are particular cases to be decided, then there is liable to be a completely unwieldy number of principles of connection. Furthermore, the fewer the principles of connection and the more general they are in their application, the more it will be possible to connect the truth of any particular judgement about which doubt is felt with many other judgements; and the more independent judgements a particular judgement can be connected with, the better will be the reasons available for deciding whether it is true or false.

Suppose we take another particular model world in order to demonstrate such principles. Suppose that this time the model world goes through a cycle of total states so that, after a certain time, the same pattern of states repeats itself. It could be taken to be in one of the three states p, q, r, for example, arranged in continual rotation so that the total states of this particular model world would be as follows:

$$p, q, r, p, q, r, p, q, r, p, q, r, p \ldots$$

Now suppose that the protagonist of this model world judged as follows:

$$\text{`}p, q, r, p, p, r, p, q, r, p, q, r, p \ldots\text{'}$$

Here the fifth judgement that he makes is false. The protagonist of this model world will be able to establish this however by means of the general principle of connection of judgements that it permits, the principle 'always "q" between "p" and "r" '. Once he uses such a principle, that is, then reasons are available enabling him to distinguish between his true and his false judgements. For in connection with his fourth and sixth judgements, he can use the principle to isolate his fifth judgement as false. Since it is a general principle he can rely on it, knowing that it is possible to give it itself independent support. He could support it in this case, for example, by using the first, second, and third judgements or by using the seventh, eighth, and ninth judgements.

Furthermore, since the principles of connection in this model world are general in their application, fewer principles are needed than there are occasions of connection. In fact, in this particular model world it is possible to express all the true connections of judgements with only two principles, for example the principle just given ('always "q" between "p" and "r" ') and the principle 'always "p" after "r" '. This not only means that it is simple to tell which is the appropriate principle on any particular occasion but also means that it is possible to connect together any judgement with any other judgement in the series. This means that it is possible for the protagonist to connect together any judgement he may feel doubt about with as many other judgements as he wishes, and so means that it is possible for him to elicit as many reasons as he desires for the truth or falsity of that particular judgement.

The principles of connection which have been given for this particular model world have been called principles of connection in judgement. Yet they obviously express how the judgements that are actually made are connected together only if the judgements that are actually made are all true. They express, that is, how the judgements have got to be if they are to be true judgements, and so make it possible to isolate the members of an actual series of judgements as true or false. Another way of putting this is that they express how the objects of judgements are connected together; if the judgements are connected in the same way then they apply to (are true of) those objects, if they are not then they do not apply to them (and so are false). It is more natural, that is, to express the principles of connection of the particular model world that were given above as applying between the total states that that world is successively in. So instead of the principles being given as 'always "q" between "p" and "r" ', with the understood rider 'if the judgements are true', they can more easily be given as 'always q between p and r'.

It is simpler and more natural to take principles of connection, therefore, as holding between the states of the world rather than as holding between the true judgements about that world. Obviously the two are equivalent in import, and so if it has been shown that the one kind of principle is necessary, then it will have been shown that the other kind of principle is necessary too. These principles of connection between states of a model world, when they are as general as the principles just given, can be called the laws of that model world. They state in a general form how that world is connected together, and so enable judgements about particular states of that world to be isolated as true or false by connecting these particular judgements with other judgements made about other states of that world.

This feature of general principles of connection has been worked out with respect to a particular model world, but this should be sufficient to show that it is a feature of the general model world. The protagonist can use the truth of some of his judgements as reasons for the truth or falsity of other of his judgements only if there are principles of connection between true judgements; these principles of connection must be general rather than particular because only then can they themselves be supported by reasons. Since they are principles of connection between true judgements, they can be taken as principles of connection between states of a world. It is a feature of the general model world, therefore, that there are general principles of connection (or laws) applying between its particular states. Or, to put it another way, the particular states of any comprehensible world must be connected together in a law-like manner.

As before, the question now arises of whether this feature has in its turn any necessary conditions for its satisfaction; and so of whether still further features may be derived from this feature. Now it is well known that any possible series of true judgements could be expressed in a law. This means that the existence of laws alone will not be sufficient to enable a protagonist to distinguish between his true judgements and his false judgements, for however unlikely a series of judgements he actually makes, it is always possible to find some law which covers that series. It also means that in a case where a judgement seemed to conflict with the law it would always be possible, instead of declaring the judgement false, to modify the law so that it covered this judgement as well. So although laws may be necessary to enable the protagonist to distinguish between his true and his false judgements, they are not by themselves sufficient to enable him to do this, and this prompts the question of whether something else may not be necessary. It seems, that is, that something else is needed if laws are going to be able to do the work that is required of them and enable a protagonist to isolate his false and his true judgements.

This something else must be a particular feature of certain

laws which enables those laws to be maintained even in the face of apparent counter-instances. For unless it is possible for the protagonist to maintain the truth of the law even when faced with an apparent counter-instance, then it is impossible for him to use the laws in the required way so that they enable him to distinguish between his true and his false judgements. For if he cannot maintain the truth of the law in the face of an apparent counter-instance, then it will be impossible for him to isolate any particular judgement as false. The laws used, therefore, must be such that they have the power to declare an apparently recalcitrant judgement false rather than being themselves changed when such a judgement appears.

The most obvious feature which would enable laws to do this would be one whereby laws varied according to their complexity, and if simpler laws were preferred to complex ones. In the particular model world already described, that is, the protagonist used the law 'always q between p and r' in order to isolate his fifth judgement as false. He could not have done this, however, on the strength of 'always q between p and r' being the only applicable law to his series of judgements. For his other judgements are equally covered by the law 'always q between p and r, except after the ten thousandth p when there is another p'; and this law would also cover his fifth judgement as being possibly true (for it might be the ten thousandth time the world wes in state p). Something more is required if the first law is to be selected as the law that operates over and above its merely being a law, and the obvious characteristic in this case is that it is the simplest law.

The idea of one law being simpler than another one is not an absolute one, since one law could seem simpler than another to one person or society and the converse be true for another person or society. It is also not possible to decide which of two laws is most simple by means of an objective test such as seeing how long it takes to write each one out in symbols or words; for different languages or symbolisms may be used or invented and different results are obviously possible between such languages or symbolisms. However, it is possible to state precisely and objectively the requirement that the feature of simplicity of laws is attempting to fulfil, and which is a requirement that must be met by every comprehensible world. This is that it must be possible for the protagonist on at least some occasions to prefer what the laws say the situation is to what he would otherwise immediately judge it to be. For if it were impossible for him to prefer the judgement derived from the laws to what he would be inclined to judge without use of the laws, then it would not be possible for him to use the laws in order to distinguish between those judgements which are true and those judgements which are false.

So it can be shown that in any comprehensible world the states of that world must be connected together in a law-like fashion so that it is possible for the protagonist of that world to use judgements he makes about some states of that world as reasons for the truth or falsity of judgements that he makes about other states of that world. These laws must be such that it is possible for the protagonist to prefer what he judges the situation to be on the basis of the law to what he would otherwise immediately judge it to be. There must therefore be some feature of laws that it would be possible for him to accept that makes it more natural for him to consider some of them as laws (and preserve in the face of apparent counter-instances) than others. This feature can be called simplicity, and the protagonist held to prefer simple laws. This, however, is not as explanatory as it might appear to be at first sight, since simplicity is not an entirely clear-cut notion.

§19 THE CASE WHERE THE PROTAGONIST IS ALWAYS RIGHT

In §15 it was remarked that a prima facie counter-example to the first premiss of this inquiry seemed to be provided by a model world in which the protagonist was always right. This seemed, that is, to be a case in which the protagonist comprehended his world and yet in which the first premiss did not apply. To test this objection, suppose that there is a particular model world in which states follow each other in an apparently totally random sequence.

$$e, s, z, r, d, x, t, f, c \ldots$$

and in which the protagonist of it appeared always to judge it correctly:

$$`e, s, z, r, d, x, t, f, c \ldots '$$

Now in this model world there would be no laws connecting together its states, and so there would be no possibility of reasons being available which could be used to isolate particular judgements as true or false. The first premiss and those other features that have been found to be required by it, that is, would not apply. Yet it seems strange to say that this particular protagonist does not understand his world. It seems sufficient for a world to be considered comprehensible, that is, that its protagonist should get all of his judgements right. Yet it seems obvious that this could happen in a world in which the first premiss is not satisfied, such as the particular model world just described. If this is so, however, the first premiss does not express a necessary condition for a world's being a comprehensible one, and neither it nor the other features found required by it would be essential features of any comprehensible world.

The objection that this particular model world illustrates is an objection to the first premiss, and so arguments derived from the first premiss cannot be used to refute it. Instead it is hoped to show that it is not as plausible as it appears, and so to add further informal support to the first premiss and the argument of the last two sections. The objection begins to seem less plausible when it is remembered that 'comprehensible' in this inquiry means 'in the same way as we comprehend', and that worlds which are to be considered comprehensible ones are worlds into which it is possible to think ourselves. So the objection illustrated by the model world just described could easily be the same type of inappropriate objection as an objection that animals comprehend (which was considered in §11). For although a world in which a protagonist gets all his judgements right seems to be a case of someone comprehending his world, just as a world in which an animal feeds itself and finds its way around seems also to be, in both cases it is difficult to see how we could think of ourselves as being in the position of the protagonist or animal unless certain other conditions are met. Yet if this is so, then getting all the judgements right is not in itself sufficient to show that someone comprehends his world. Certain other features are necessary; and these may well be the features demonstrated in the last three sections.

This way of answering the objection is reinforced if it is

suggested that the vital question has already been begged in the way that the particular model world was described at the beginning of this section. For, from the strictly outside point of view in which this model world is seen as created in the context of our present world, it is hard to see how the protagonist's judgements can be described as having the particular values that they do have. What happens is that there is some feature of the protagonist that varies in each case. It could be shown that this feature was always the same when the state of the world was the same; but more than this would need to be shown if this feature were to be taken as correct judgement about that state of the world. For this feature might just be some feature of the protagonist whose variation was caused by the external world in the way that the sun causes a sunshine recorder to vary in its readings; yet a recorder could not be said to judge how the sun is, nor to comprehend its world.

Without examining precisely what is required from the external point of view in order to say that someone or something is judging, it can be summed up by saying that it must be possible for us who are studying him or it to think of ourselves as being in the place of the person or thing we are studying. This is why the model worlds are developed with a protagonist who is taken to be judging; it is because they are developed with a position into which it is possible to think ourselves. The model world given at the beginning of this section must not only be looked at from the external position, therefore, but also from the internal (or protagonist's own) position. However, once it is looked at from this position it can be seen that it lacks certain essential features of any comprehensible world. For it is clear that in this world no distinction is possible for someone inside it between getting his judgements right and getting them wrong. It would be exactly the same from the inside if the same series of judgements were made and if they were all wrong instead of all right. There is nothing available on the inside to distinguish between getting a judgement right or wrong, and so nothing to demonstrate what a false judgement would be like and nothing that gives any grounds for calling any of the judgements true.

The objection examined in this section rests on the idea

that the truth of the judgements someone makes is an important factor in determining whether someone understands his world. This is taken by the objection to be such an important factor that it alone is sufficient to say whether anyone judges or not. However, the objection forgets that more is required if such a person is to be taken to be judging in the first place and that, in particular, it must be possible for this person himself to think of his judgements as being true, rather than their just being declared true from an external position. If the person is to be taken to be judging at all, that is, then he must be thought of as selecting some judgements as true rather than others; he must be taken to be giving some weight to the quality of truth-aimedness which is an essential feature of judgement. Yet in the kind of case visualized by the objection, there is no possibility of such selection, for there are none of the things that have been found to be required if such a selection is to be possible, such as connection between logically independent judgements and laws. The emphasis that the objection puts on truth turns against it, for in the case envisaged by the objection no difference can be made between truth and falsity nor can it be said what a false judgement would be like.

Another way of bringing out this point is to point out that in this particular model world, when viewed from the point of view of its protagonist, there is no difference between a judgement being different and the world being different. If, for example, the protagonist of this world judges 'c, but it might have been z', there is no difference for him between taking this as applying to the possibility of his having made another judgement (and so a wrong one) and taking this as applying to the possibility of the world having been different. There is no question of taking judgements as applying or as not applying to the world, that is; no question of them being thought of as true or false. Which is another way of saying that such a protagonist could not be taken to be making judgements at all.

A similar reply can be given to the objection mentioned at the beginning of §17, the objection that the reasons available to the protagonist might not be expressible as judgements. From the outside position this again looks at first sight as if it is a perfectly good objection. There must be some difference to the protagonist between the cases in which he judges something truly and the cases in which he judges something falsely; but there seems no reason why this difference should be something available to him to be judged, and therefore expressible as judgements. It seems that it could, for example, be some factor in his physical constitution that he was never conscious of. This factor would be causally responsible for him being able to distinguish between true and false judgements, and so would be causally responsible for him getting the right answer most of the time. Yet, in that he would not be conscious of such a factor, it could not be a possible object of his judgements. So from the outside position it seems to be a perfectly sound objection that the reasons available to the protagonist might not be expressible as judgements.

This objection is similar to the previous one, however, in that it is again the case that, from the protagonist's point of view, there is no difference at all between making a false judgement and making a true one. Although, that is, we could observe from the outside the causal factors that were influencing his judgement, as long as the protagonist was held to be wholly unaware of such factors, then what it was like to make true judgements for him is exactly like what it was like to make false judgements. Unless the causal factors were available to him as well as to us, then he can make no distinction between judgements applying to the world and judgements not applying to the world. Just as before, unless he can do this, then he cannot distinguish between a change in the judgements and a change in the world; and so cannot be taken to be making judgements at all. So just as before, once the inside position is considered, it can be seen that not only must the protagonist be able to make true judgements but reasons must also be available to him enabling him to do so; and it can be seen that not only must someone be able to observe these reasons but that the protagonist himself must be able to observe them, which means that these reasons must be expressible as judgements of his. This supports the first premiss and the first deductions from it: reasons must be available to the protagonist, and these reasons will not be available to him unless they are expressible as judgements of his.

In the model worlds given in the last section, in which it

is possible for the protagonist to connect together his judgements, the situation is quite different from the suggested
cases of this section which can only be made sense of from the
outside position. For in them the protagonist can easily distinguish between his judgements as being true or false; he
can represent to himself what it would be like to make a false
judgement; and he can distinguish between the world having
been different and his having made another judgement. In
the model worlds discussed in the last sections, that is, it is
possible to give scope to the idea of truth, and of the quality
of truth-aimedness involved in judgement, on the inside position (that is, from the protagonist's point of view). This means
that the protagonist can be taken to be judging, and it is
precisely some of the necessary conditions for this that have
been worked out in the last two sections.

Both these two objections just considered, therefore, fail
to show that the first premiss and the features that have been
found to be required by that premiss are not essential conditions of a world being comprehensible. For the feature that
the first objection relied on, the truth (viewed from the
external position) of the protagonist's judgements, is not in
itself sufficient for us to consider that protagonist as comprehending. It is also essential that he can be thought of as
making judgements, and for this it must be possible to make
some distinction between truth and falsity on the inside position as well. For this it is essential that reasons, and reasons
expressible as judgements, are available to him. Yet this is
exactly what the first premiss demands. These objections,
therefore, do not work against the necessity of the feature
premised in the first premiss nor against the other features
found to be required by this first feature.

It should be noticed that an inquiry such as the present
one is concerned with necessary conditions rather than sufficient ones. It is only claimed that the first premiss supplies a
necessary condition of a world being comprehensible, not a
sufficient one; and the other features derived from the premiss
are similarly only necessary conditions, not sufficient ones.
It is not, therefore, claimed that a world in which there is
a law-like connection, and so in which reasons can be given for
the truth of judgements, contains sufficient features to make
that world a comprehensible one. For, as Descartes realized

while developing his fiction of a *malin genie* who could always be deceiving us, it would be quite possible for the protagonist of a model world to link together all his judgements in a law-like fashion and yet for all his judgements (as we on the outside of that world would be able to declare) to be wrong.

Someone who is fooled by a Cartesian *malin genie* could not be said to comprehend his world, although he is more likely to be said to miscomprehend it than not to comprehend it at all. This is the correct insight which lies behind the objection examined in this section. It does seem, that is, to be a necessary condition of a person's being considered as comprehending his world that he gets most of his judgements about it right. Yet this section has shown that it is not a sufficient condition, and that there are other necessary conditions of a world being a comprehensible one, such as those derived in the previous sections. Of course these conditions are only necessary ones, yet it is just such necessary conditions that the present inquiry is attempting to discover. The objection considered in this section, therefore, does not tell against the first premiss and the subsequent derivations from it.

§20 ALTERNATIVE PREMISSES

The first premiss to the inquiry, which has been given further informal support in the last section, led to some interesting results in §§17 and 18. In particular, it was found to involve the requirement that the states of any comprehensible world must be connected together in law-like fashion, enabling judgements about certain of these states to form reasons for the truth or falsity of judgements about other of these states. This conclusion is obviously similar to some of Kant's conclusions in the *Critique of Pure Reason*. This makes it interesting to compare the argument and premiss of this inquiry with the argument and premiss used by Kant. It is impossible here to indulge in detailed exegesis, but it is possible to give one or two arguments which are interesting in their own right and which Kant may have meant. The aim is to see whether there is a valid alternative starting-point to the first premiss of this inquiry, or whether other starting points depend upon this first premiss and so are less fundamental than it.

In the part of the *Critique* known as the 'Transcendental Deduction' it seems clear that the argument starts from what Kant calls the transcendental unity of apperception. The idea Kant seems to be relying on is that, since all my representations are *my* representations, they must all in some way be connected with me, and that this unifies them:

> The unity of this apperception I likewise entitle the *transcendental* unity of self-consciousness, in order to indicate the possibility of *a priori* knowledge arising from it. For the manifold representations, which are given in an intuition, would not be one and all *my* representations, if they did not all belong to one self-consciousness. As *my* representations (even if I am not conscious of them as such) they must conform to the condition under which alone they *can* stand together in one universal self-consciousness, because otherwise they would not all without exception belong to me. From this original combination many consequences follow. (B132–3).

Kant's aim here seems to be to argue from the tautology that all my representations are my representations, and this passage quoted leads one to suspect that consequences can be derived from such a premiss by seeing what conditions must be fulfilled if representations are to be able to do this. These consequences may, at least, be taken to be the synthesis of the manifold of judgements and of the objects judged which the Transcendental Deduction aims to demonstrate. If this is so, Kant seems to be able to provide an argument to some of the conclusions argued for above (specifically the connection of judgements and of objects judged) while using a different, and apparently even more fundamental, premiss.

It is difficult, however, to see what this argument is. It might be suggested that all the judgements which were united by being judged by one self-consciousness were therefore united in themselves. It might be suggested, that is, that judgements could not be united in the way they have to be to be judged by one person unless there was something about the content of the judgements themselves which would unite them. Yet it is not obvious why this should be thought to be so. On the contrary, it does not seem possible to lay down, *a priori*, any conditions which a judgement needs to fulfil in order to be a judgement of mine; the situation is rather that it is presupposed that all judgements are somebody's judgements. In a situation in which I was the only person in it, therefore, it would be presupposed that all judgements were mine; just as in a particular model world in which only a protagonist makes judgements, it is presupposed that all judgements are judgements of his. It does not seem, therefore, that any conditions are laid on the contents of judgements by their being judgements of mine, or of one particular person. This is not to say that certain conditions will not have to apply in judgement of any actual case, such as judgement of the present world, if two judgements are going to be taken as being made by the same person. These conditions, however, arise from the nature of that particular world and not just because the two judgements are made by one person. For example, in our present situation, two simultaneous aural judgements of widely separated sources of sound cannot be taken to be both judgements of one person. This, however, is because one person cannot be in two widely separated places simultaneously in our world and because sound only travels a certain distance in it. It is not because there are conditions which apply just because two judgements are made by one person. The conditions in this case, that is, are conditions imposed by being judgements of a world, not conditions arising out of that judgement being the judgement of one person.

The requirement that '*my* representations . . . must conform to the condition under which alone they *can* stand together in one universal self-consciousness', therefore, although it is an extremely fundamental requirement and worthy on that account to be assumed as the first premiss, does not seem to provide any conditions or lead to any further features in the way that the first premiss has succeeded in doing. In particular, it does not seem that it would lead to the conclusion that there must be laws and connection between logically independent judgements. Kant, however, took this requirement as equivalent to, or at least as implying, the quite different requirement that all my representations 'must be subject to that condition under which alone I can ascribe them to the identical self as *my* representations' (B138). In this he is supported by Strawson, who remarks on p. 98 of *The Bounds of Sense* that 'unity of the consciousness to which a series of experiences belongs implies . . . the possibility of self-ascription of experiences on the part of a subject of those experiences.' This is a quite different requirement because, although it is obvious that two judgements could not be judgements of one person without fulfilling the conditions of two judgements being judgements of one person, it is not at all obvious that one of these conditions is that he has to be able to say that they are both judgements of *his*. The first requirement does not imply the second.

It might be suggested that even though this second requirement does not follow from the first, it should be adopted in its own right as a first premiss to the inquiry. It seems, also, that if it were interesting consequences might follow from it similar to those which Strawson derives in the third chapter of *Individuals*. The objection to this, however, is that it is too weak a premiss to form the fundamental premiss of an inquiry such as the present. It is just not obvious enough that, in any comprehensible world, a person judging that world must be able to isolate his judgements as being *his* judgements and to judge that they are *his* judgements. It is much more obvious that a person judging such a world must be able to distinguish between his true and his false judgements. So the first premiss which has been adopted is clearly preferable to this suggested alternative.

Furthermore, although adoption of this premiss would lead to interesting consequences, it does not look as if it would lead to the features derived from the present first premiss, and which Kant took himself to have demonstrated in the *Critique of Pure Reason*. So even if the first suggested requirement is taken (erroneously) to imply the second suggested requirement, it still has to be explained how either of them could lead to these features. The first requirement seems to lead to no features at all, and the second to different features. If, however, the second requirement (all my representations 'must be subject to that condition under which alone I can ascribe them to the identical self as *my* representations') is not taken, as above, to be expressing the claim that I must be able to tell that my representations are *my* representations, but instead is taken as expressing the claim that I must be able to tell which, out of a group of possible representations, were the ones I really had, then it seems that an argument similar to those of previous sections would emerge. It only seems possible to make an argument which results in the features derived in the last sections from something like Kant's starting-point, that is, if instead of asking what conditions representations presumed to be mine must meet in order to be my representations, or in order to be self-ascribed as mine, it is asked what conditions possible representations must meet if I am going to be able to isolate among those possible representations those which I actually had. This is the way that Bennett understands Kant in his exegesis. He remarks in *Kant's Analytic*: 'Although it is only in special circumstances that I can know that someone had a certain mental state and wonder whether it was I, there is nothing special about the case where I wonder whether a past mental state was mine *by* wondering whether it existed at all' (p. 118), and so argues that: 'Self-consciousness, then, involves whatever intellectual capacities may be required for the establishment . . . of the truth of statements about one's own past mental states' (p. 119).

If Kant's premiss is taken in this way it is easy to see that it generates a real argument in which the required capacities can be discovered. These capacities will turn out to be the ones enshrined in the features already derived in the general model world. Yet this is not because these features can be derived from a different, and possibly more fundamental, premiss. It is because if Kant's premiss is understood in this way it is only a special case of the first premiss used in the present inquiry. For if it is understood in this way it requires that someone should be able to tell which mental states he had in the past. This is to require that someone should be able to distinguish between true and false judgements about his past mental states, which is a special case of requiring that someone should be able to distinguish between true and false judgements, which is (part of) the first premiss. So although something like the features already derived can be derived from this premiss, this is only because it is a special case of the original first premiss. It does not therefore pose a rival to it.

It seems, therefore, as if an alternative, more fundamental, premiss cannot be discovered by looking at Kant's argument. For although Kant's argument arrives at similar conclusions to the conclusions of §§17 and 18, the only interpretation of a Kantian premiss on which it does this is an interpretation which makes it a special case of the present first premiss. It should also be remarked that this is an interpretation for which there is not much textual support in the Transcendental Deduction. The first and second interpretations have much more textual support. Yet it has been seen that the first interpretation involves a feature which does not look as if it leads to any further features at all, and that the second interpretation involves too weak a feature to be adopted as the fundamental premiss of an inquiry such as the present one. So although Kant's Transcendental Deduction appears to have a conclusion similar to the requirement argued for above that there should be connection between logically independent judgements, there does not seem to be in it a premiss from which such a conclusion could be derived, and which would form a rival to the present first premiss.

If the Transcendental Deduction has a conclusion similar to §17 (that there must be connection between logically independent judgements), the Second Analogy has a conclusion similar to §18 (that there must be laws, or general principles of connection between judgements). Yet in so far as the Second Analogy is not just taken as an application of the Transcendental Deduction to a particular subject matter and is held to be an independent argument with its own premisses, it also does not seem to produce any rival premiss to the present first premiss. For the premiss it most naturally can be taken to depend upon is that it must be possible to determine the order of representations in time. This, again, is merely a special case of the first premiss since it is the requirement that it must be possible for a judger to tell at what times the states of affairs he judges occur, which in turn is the requirement that the protagonist must be able to distinguish between those judgements of his about the time at which something occurs which are true and those judgements of his about the time at which something occurs which are false. This is obviously a special case of the first premiss. This alone would make it inferior; however, it is also inferior in that it would depend on the questionable assumption that any comprehensible world must contain not only time but also judgements about time. Although it has not been possible to indulge in detailed exegesis, therefore, it does not seem as if there is in Kant a premiss which is both more fundamental that the present first premiss and which would also be a preferable alternative to it.

Another alternative premiss that might be suggested is that used by Strawson when constructing his world of sounds in Chapter Two of *Individuals*. This is that it must be possible for someone to distinguish between states of himself and states not of himself. Yet again this seems less fundamental than the premiss used above. For whereas it does not seem possible to think of the protagonist as judging at all, nor possible to think of ourselves in any way in his position, if there is no possibility of distinguishing between true and false judgements, it does seem possible to think of a protagonist not distinguishing between (as they might be called) inner and outer states. If, for example, there are no other people in his world, there seems no reason why he should distinguish between judgements of inner states and judgements of outer states; yet even if there are no other people in his world he must be taken to be able to select between true and false judgements, if he is to be taken as judging at all. It may well, that is, be impossible for someone to comprehend his world unless he can distinguish between states of himself and states not of himself. This, however, is not obvious and so needs to be demonstrated by argument rather than just assumed as a premiss.

This premiss used by Strawson, therefore, is not one that could be used in the present inquiry. It is mentioned here because of the possibility of confusion between it and the first premiss. This arises because it is possible to call the distinction insisted on in both cases the objective-subjective distinction; even though quite a different distinction is demanded by the two premisses. Strawson, for example, calls states which are outer and objects of experiences (inner states) 'objective particulars' as the following quotation shows:

The limit I want to impose on my general question is this: that I intend it as a question about the conditions of the possibility of identifying thought about particulars distinguished by the thinker from himself and from his own experiences or states of mind, and regarded as actual or possible *objects* of those experiences. I shall henceforth use the phrase 'objective particulars' as an abbreviation of the entire phrase 'particulars distinguished by the thinker &c.' (p. 61).

So it would be possible for him to call the distinction between states of oneself and states not of oneself the subjective-objective distinction. However it is also possible to call the distinction between those beliefs or judgements which are true, or at least well grounded, and those beliefs which only appear to be true, or are not well grounded, the objective-subjective distinction. For example, on the first use of the distinction, when I judge that I have a headache, this is a subjective judgement, and when I judge that I can see a table this is an objective judgement. On the second use of the distinction, it is an objective judgement when I judge that I had a headache yesterday if this judgement is well grounded (I could produce good reasons for its truth); whereas when I judge that I saw a table here yesterday, this is a subjective judgement if it is not well grounded (if I could produce no good reasons for its truth).

In that it is possible to call both premisses the assertion of the objective–subjective distinction, it is therefore possible that the two premisses could get confused and one derive the plausibility that was only deserved by the other. However, once this possibility of confusion is mentioned it can clearly be seen that the premiss used as a first premiss in the present inquiry is more fundamental than the present suggested alternative premiss. The first premiss is not identical with any premiss about the inner-outer distinction, nor does it have any obvious direct bearing on the inner-outer distinction. The study of alternative premisses, therefore, carried out in this section, reinforces the fundamental nature of the first premiss that has been chosen. Copiously demonstrated informally, and also with respect to potential rivals, it may be regarded as well secured. Once it is so regarded, then an equal certainty attaches to the results that were seen to follow from it in §§17 and 18.

CHAPTER FOUR

Time

§21 NECESSITY OF SPACE OR TIME

IT is natural to assume that it is an extremely fundamental property of any comprehensible world that it should contain time. This is something which is normally assumed without question; and when it is argued for, as in Kant, it is argued for in a perfunctory manner. It is something which it seems that there could be no disagreement about. It is something, therefore, which it would be safe to introduce into the general model world by means of a second premiss.

Before resorting to a second premiss, however, it is interesting to see whether it might not be possible to derive time from the features of the general model world which have already been derived in the last chapter. If it can be derived it will provide a justification for time that is usually lacking. If it cannot, it will provide a much better insight into the nature of time and the role that it plays in our comprehension of the world than would be provided by assuming it straight off without argument. In either case it will demonstrate how it is possible to argue for an extremely fundamental feature. It will also provide an opportunity to try out the techniques of Chapter Two on uncontroversial subject matter before they are used in the contested areas which follow.

In §17 it was concluded that the protagonist of the general model world must be able to connect together his individual judgements so that the truth of some of them formed reasons for the truth or falsity of others of them. In §18 it was seen that this required general principles of connection so that, in any comprehensible world, the objects of judgements must be connected together in a general and law-like manner. These laws give a general expression of how the objects are connected together in several particular cases. The typical law 'whenever x, then y', for example, expresses what happens in all those particular cases in which there is an x. Now such laws only have point if they do apply to several instances;

for, as was argued in §18, the point of the laws is to provide support for the judgement of an instance over and above what can be provided by the judgement of the instance itself. In order for such laws to be used, therefore, it must be possible for the protagonist to distinguish between different instances in which the same pairs of properties (the same kinds of objects) are conjoined. He must be able to distinguish, for example, between several different cases in which x is associated with y if he is going to be able to use the general law 'whenever x, then y'. So the protagonist can use laws to distinguish between his true and his false judgements only if he can distinguish between the several different instances which fall under each law.

The only general methods known to us by which several instances in which the same properties are conjoined may be distinguished from one another are the use of space and the use of time. Two instances, that is, in which x is associated with y may be distinguished from each other if they occur at different times or at different places. If, therefore, it could be shown that these were the only methods of separation that there were, then it would have been shown that the general model world must contain either space or time.

Since it is difficult to show that these are the only methods by which two similar instances can be distinguished from one another, the necessity of space or time must remain a tentative conclusion. What can be shown, however, is that apparently plausible alternative means of making a distinction will not do so unless they presuppose space and time. For example, it might be suggested that two occasions in which x was associated with y might be distinguished from one another because one of them was an occasion in which they were both associated with, for example, u and v, while the other of them was an occasion in which they were both associated with w and z. This suggestion, however, will not do the work that is required of it, because it presupposes that it is possible to tell, for example, that $u, v, x,$ and y are associated with each other on a single occasion. Yet it is just how to tell what is associated with what on a single occasion that is under discussion and to which this suggestion was supposed to provide an answer.

It does no good, that is, to distinguish between two occasions in which x and y are associated with each other by seeing that one of them is an occasion in which they are associated with u and v unless it is possible to distinguish between two occasions in which u, v, x, and y are associated with each other. The same problem comes up again, and so another method (such as the use of either space or time) must be used at some stage in order to prevent a regress. It might be thought, however, that the regress could be stopped quite properly by the assumption that there was just one instance in which any particular complex of properties were associated with one another. Yet this would still not provide an alternative means to the use of either space or time. For this assumption depends on being able to tell what is a single instance of combination. Yet it is exactly how to tell which combinations of properties constitute instances that is at the heart of the question; and it is exactly this question which can be answered if we are allowed to suppose the existence of either time or space in a world. If there is either time or space, combinations of properties can be taken as constituting instances when they appear together, that is when they appear at the same time or the same space.

It seems, that is, that either time or space is necessary in any world in which it is possible to have the idea of an individual object of judgement, and in which it is possible to distinguish between two different cases of the same kind of judgement. Yet it has been shown that the protagonist of the general model world must be able to distinguish between different instances of judgement, and in particular between different instances in which the same properties are combined. So it seems that either time or space is another feature of the general model world at this level. This can only be a tentative conclusion since all the alternatives to time and space have not been considered, and since the argument about time or space itself has been rather schematic. However, it should increase our confidence in our ability to derive time as a feature of the general model world at this level. For if either time or space is required, it need only be shown that space alone is insufficient in order to show the necessity of time.

On the other hand, if either time or space seems to be required, the most convincing proof that time alone is required would be to take a world that already contained space and to show that, nevertheless, it must also contain time. This is the method which will be followed in this chapter. A particular model world which explicitly contains space, but does not explicitly contain time, will be taken, and it will then be seen whether it lacks a feature which is essential in any comprehensible world. If there is such a feature, it will have been shown that an atemporal world is an incomprehensible one and that time is a feature of any comprehensible world. It will have been shown that not only is either time or space essential (if this is indeed the case) but that time alone is. The argument does not depend upon this section, and will be much more rigorous and precise.

§22   PARTICULAR MODEL WORLD TO DERIVE TIME

It has been decided to take a particular model world which contains space but does not, at least explicitly, contain time, and to see whether this world lacks an essential feature of all comprehensible worlds. It must be shown, that is, that this world could not possess some feature which either has been already derived in the construction of the general model world or which can be derived in its construction. The particular model world which will be used for this purpose is a world in which, as we on the outside of it would say, nothing ever changes. This particular model world represents the formal structure of an atemporal world, and if it could not possess some feature possessed by the general model world, then it will have been shown that the general model world must contain time.

There is no change in this particular model world. Its protagonist, therefore, must be thought of as making all his judgements simultaneously. The instances judged will be distinguished by spatial rather than temporal means, and so the laws used to connect together instances of judgement will be spatial rather than temporal in form. Instead, that is, of declaring that two kinds of thing are associated at the same times ('whenever x, then y'), they will declare that two kinds of thing are associated at the same places ('wherever x, then y'). The protagonist will use such spatial laws in order to distinguish between his true and his false judgements, and in order to support what he judges in one particular instance by means of what he judges in other instances. Since he must make all his judgements (as we on the outside would say) simultaneously, not only all his direct judgements about the world, but also his reasons for the support of those judgements and his use of the laws of the world must all be judged (as we would say) at the same time.

Since there is no change in this model world, there can be no change in the reasons available to the protagonist which enable him to isolate a particular judgement as true or false. There can also be no change in his opinion about a particular judgement, so that a judgement he takes as true will always be true for him. He must think of himself, therefore, as the final authority about his world. This is not to say that he could not conceive of his judgements being false. He could not, however, ever be in possession of sufficient reasons for the falsity of one of his judgements. For since he is immediately in possession of all the reasons that any judgement could have for him in that world, if he had had possession of such sufficient reasons, he would have judged otherwise than he did. From the protagonist's point of view, therefore, it is idle to suppose that any of his judgements might be false. He might, of course, not be certain whether a particular judgement was true or not; but it is idle for him to suppose that any judgement he definitely takes as true might actually be false.

Perhaps an analogy will help in visualizing this particular model world. In it the protagonist holds all his judgements and all the reasons for those judgements simultaneously. This can be compared to a page in a mathematics book. On such a page there is a complete argument with one line of proof being used as a reason for the next line, yet all the lines exist simultaneously on the page. This protagonist's judgements are like this: every judgement he makes is thought of as existing simultaneously for him in the way that the lines of proof on the page exist simultaneously. The protagonist is like, therefore, a man who takes in a whole page of mathematics in a single glance. If it can be shown in any way that the judgements required in a comprehensible world can not be thought of as existing simultaneously in the way that the lines of proof on a page can be thought of as existing simultaneously, this will show that a comprehensible atemporal world is impossible.

The particular model world that is being used has been

described in terms of time. This, however, is only the description of the model world from our own position on the outside of it and in a temporal world. The point of using this particular model world is that none of the judgements made by the protagonist involve time. Even though it itself is described in temporal terms, therefore, it can be used to examine the features of an atemporal world. If this world in which all the protagonist's judgements are made simultaneously is excluded by the first premiss and features derived from it, this will show that an atemporal world could not possess certain features required by any comprehensible world. Although it is described by us in temporal terms, it will have been used to demonstrate that an atemporal world would be an incomprehensible world.

§23 ATTEMPTS TO SHOW THIS WORLD INCOMPREHENSIBLE

It was seen in the last section that in this particular model world the protagonist cannot change his mind about a judgement, and so it is for him as if he gets all his judgements correct. His position in this respect is analogous to the case of a protagonist who never makes a mistake, such as was dealt with in §19. In the same way as described there, this will not in itself make the world incomprehensible for this protagonist. It is still possible for him to represent to himself what it would be like to make a mistake, if this is felt to be required. For he could imagine having the same reasons available as he does at present and yet by some inexplicable accident holding the wrong judgement, a judgement that they did not support. The protagonist could imagine judging this simultaneously with the correct judgement, with the judgement that was supported by the available evidence. His total judgement, for example, might be: 'a, but I could have judged b; it is a though, because of reasons x, y, z.' So even if it is held that the protagonist of a comprehensible world must know what false judgements are like, which has not been shown to follow from the first premiss, there is no requirement here that could not be met by this particular model world.

So if a feature is to be found which any comprehensible world must possess and which this particular world does not possess, it must be found elsewhere. Another candidate is that the protagonist of any comprehensible world must be able to know things beyond his immediate experience. This could be put in the form that he must be able to judge things indirectly (depending upon other judgements) that he could not judge directly (depending upon no other judgements). For it might seem at first that this feature could not be possessed by the particular model world, in that it is impossible for its protagonist to revise his judgements and to discover new things about the world. This seems a sharp contrast from our present situation in this world in which we are able to make many judgements about how the world is which go beyond our present experience, since we can rely upon our experience at other times. However, on further reflection, it seems that the protagonist of this particular model world could judge beyond his experience, or at least could judge indirectly things that he could not judge directly. For there is no reason why he could not use the laws of his world to spread the force of the judgements that he can make directly to certain judgements that he can only make indirectly. Just as the laws can be used to support and correct judgements of immediate experience, they can be used to support or initiate judgements which go beyond experience. Possessed, therefore, of laws, the protagonist can make judgements which go beyond his experience. There is nothing here that he could not do simultaneously, and so, even if it could be shown that this suggested feature follows from the features demonstrated already, it is a feature which could be possessed by an atemporal world.

A better candidate for the required formal feature is that the protagonist could know more than he does know. It seems that this could not be a feature of an atemporal world simply because an atemporal protagonist's knowledge of his world cannot change. However, again it is not so obvious on further reflection that an atemporal world (or that the particular model world) could not possess the feature in question. For although the protagonist's knowledge of this particular world could not change, it seems possible to say that he might have had a different knowledge of it. For example, he might have been in a different place from the one he now occupies and so able to make different direct judgements about the world from the ones he makes at present. Yet if he had been at such a different place it is reasonable to suppose not just that different of his judgements would be direct, but also that he would have different knowledge of the whole world. This knowledge might well be greater than the knowledge he possesses at present, for it might well be the case that this new position enabled more of the laws of the model world to be discovered and so enabled more inferences to be made. Since, therefore, the protagonist could have been in a different position in this model world, it is possible that he could have known more than he does know. It is not, therefore, so obvious as it appears at first sight to be that the feature that the protagonist could know more about his world than he does know could not be possessed by this particular model world.

It can be objected that the feature that the protagonist could know more than he does know is not at all the same thing as the feature that the protagonist could have known more than he does know. In the light of this objection, a formal feature will shortly be produced which it is impossible for any atemporal world to possess. This feature, however, cannot just be that it is possible that the protagonist knows more than he at present knows. For the protagonist could have been at a different place in the world; he could have had a different ability to connect judgements; or he could have been able to make more direct judgements from any place than he can at present. In any of these ways he would have been able to know more than he does at present know, and so the possibility of him knowing more than he does know follows from the possibility of these ways. Since, that is, it is contingent where the protagonist is, or how well he can connect judgements together, or how many direct judgements he can make from any one position, it seems that any of these things could be different; in which case the protagonist could know more than he does know.

The confusion about whether the latest suggested feature could be possessed by the particular model world depends upon a tangle in the idea of possibility which is being used. In one sense it seems clear that the protagonist could not know more than he does know, since it is impossible for anything in the world to change, including the protagonist's knowledge. Yet on the other hand it seems equally clear that since it is only contingent that the world is as it is, it could easily have been otherwise. With this in mind it looks as though the particular model world might after all be able to possess the feature in question. So the simplest way to clear this confusion up is to take instead the feature that the protagonist must be able to know in that world more than he does know in that world. This feature is much more clearly one which no atemporal world could possess. Yet it still allows that it is contingent that the protagonist is where he is or as he is, for this contingency now becomes the contingency that it is this world which exists rather than another one. Whereas it is not possible, that is, for the protagonist to be somewhere else in that world (and so not possible for him to know more than he does know in that world), it is possible that a world existed which was similar to that one except for the position in it of the protagonist. So if the feature that the protagonist could know more than he does know in that particular world he is in is taken as the feature to be considered, it is a feature which the particular model world (and so no atemporal world) could possess. If, that is, it can be shown that this feature follows from the features already derived from the first premiss, then it will have been shown that an atemporal world is an incomprehensible one.

§24 ARGUMENT FOR THE SUGGESTED FEATURE

It will be remembered that the general strategy of this chapter is to find some feature which could not be possessed by any atemporal world, and then to attempt to show that this feature can be derived from the first premiss and the features found to be required by it. In the last section, a feature emerged which it was clear could not be possessed by an atemporal world. The object of this section, therefore, is to see whether this feature can be derived from the other features of any comprehensible world which were derived in the last chapter.

The first premiss to the whole inquiry, enunciated in §15, is that reasons must be available to the protagonist enabling him to distinguish between those of the judgements he might make which are true, and those which are false. As remarked in §17, and supported in §19, these reasons will themselves be expressible as judgements. If they are to fulfil the requirement of the first premiss, therefore, they will themselves need reasons with which it is possible to distinguish between their truth and their falsity. These reasons in turn, themselves being further judgements, will require still further reasons. So if the first premiss is to be fulfilled, the protagonist of a comprehensible world does not merely need reasons available to him with which to decide the truth or the falsity of his judgements, but an infinity of such reasons. For any reason which is available will in turn demand another reason being available with which its truth or falsity may be determined. There is no natural position at which this process can end; and so an infinity of reasons must be available to the protagonist.

Although at first sight this seems to be a startling result, it is easy to see that it is fulfilled in our present world. For it only implies that we can go back as far as we want along the chain of reasons; could always, that is, produce another reason if we felt it to be necessary. The infinity of reasons does not need to be actual, but may be merely potential. The infinity is merely potential because there is no need for there actually to exist an infinite number of reasons nor (*a fortiori*) for any-one actually to possess an infinite number of reasons. All that is necessary is that an infinite number of reasons are available, so that someone may always have access to another reason apart from the ones he already has whenever he should require it. This means that in our own present world, the infinity of reasons required is not an actual infinity but merely a potential one; and this is why it is possible for there to be an infinity of reasons available in our own present world.

The requirement that an infinity of reasons be available to the protagonist does not seem to be as easy to meet in an atemporal world as it is in our own present world, however. For in an atemporal world, this contrast between potentiality and actuality does not exist; and if so an atemporal protago-nist is to possess the reasons in question he must possess them all (as we on the outside would say) simultaneously. So the atemporal protagonist, such as the protagonist of the par-ticular model world described in §22, would need to have an actual infinity of reasons if he is to satisfy the first premiss of the inquiry.

A feature of any comprehensible world, therefore, is that at least a potential infinity of reasons are available to the pro-tagonist of that world. Yet the way in which such an infinity can occur differs markedly between an atemporal and a temporal world. In an atemporal world, which cannot possess the feature that its protagonist could know in that world more than he does know in that world, all that the protagonist does know must be known by him (as we on the outside would say) at once. So the only way in which such an infinity can occur in an atemporal world is as an actual infinity of judgements. In a temporal world such as our own, by contrast, the infinity can be merely potential since all that is required is that reasons could always be elicited if they ever should be wanted; the reasons only need to be available, they do not need to be present.

If it can be assumed, therefore, that the possession of an actual infinity of judgements or reasons by a protagonist is impossible, or impossible in a comprehensible world, then this would mean that the atemporal world would be eliminated by the developed premiss. For a feature would have been found to follow from this premiss which could not be possessed in any atemporal world. This is the feature that the protagonist could know in that world more than he does know in it. This feature follows from the developed premiss once it is assumed that it is impossible for a protagonist to possess an actual infinity of reasons, for the infinity of reasons that the first premiss requires can then only be a potential infinity, which implies that the protagonist for which they were potential reasons could know in that world more than he does know in that world.

However, the assumption that an actual infinity of reasons is impossible is not at all obvious. If it were possible it would imply that it would be possible for a protagonist to have an infinitely large intellect, and it is possible to give some picture of what this would be like. For it would be possible to imagine a particular model world in which, as before, the protagonist held all his judgements simultaneously and in which it was also the case that, however many of his judgements we described or repeated on the outside of his world, it was still the case that there were other judgements that he held. If, for example, the judgements in question were reasons for a particular judgement, and the reasons for those reasons, then it might be the case that all the judgements that we would give as reasons if we had to elicit them were exactly the

judgements that were judged simultaneously by this protagonist. And in that the reasons we could give need not,
indeed must not, come to an end, so also could the judgements
of the protagonist that correspond to the judgements we give
be limitless. So one flaw in the above argument is that the
assumption that it rests on, the assumption that there could
not be an actual infinity of reasons, is not at all obvious.

It is also not certain that the first bit of the above argument
works. For though the first premiss implies that a potential
infinity of reasons must exist, in that further reasons must
always be available if desired, it may be the case that this, after
all, could be satisfied in an atemporal world like the particular model world of §22. It was assumed above that it
could not, since it was assumed that it was pointless to say that
there were reasons for something unless it was actually possible to give those reasons. If, therefore, there must be an
infinite number of reasons for something, it was correspond-
ingly assumed that either they all had to be already given or
else it had to be possible to produce them. Only the first
alternative would be possible in an atemporal world and so
it was assumed that the protagonist of an atemporal world
would have to be in possession of an actual infinity of reasons
if that world were to be comprehensible.

On further reflection, however, it appears that the first
premiss is satisfied if the protagonist knows that reasons are
available and that it is unnecessary for these reasons actually
to be produced. If, for example, a protagonist knew that,
however many reasons were produced, they would all support
each other and his original judgement, then he would not
actually have to produce those reasons. Here the protagonist
would be using the reasons that were available in order to
distinguish between his true judgements and his false judgements, yet he would not actually be producing the reasons.
If this is possible, then a potential infinity of judgements and
reasons could be available to the protagonist which he could
use to support the truth of some of his judgements without
him ever having to specify or produce those reasons. Yet if
he can do this, then the potential infinity of reasons demanded
by the first premiss could exist and be used by the protagonist
without implying either that the protagonist has an infinitely
large intellect (to contain all the reasons) or that time is

present in the world (so that the required reasons can be given as far as, and whenever, necessary).

It might seem that reasons could not be known to exist which would support the truth of a judgement unless it was either the case that those reasons had already been given (which leads to an actual infinity of judgements and an infinitely large intellect) or the case that such reasons could be given if required (which leads to time). Take the case, however, in which the reasons that a set of judgements provided for each other were circular in nature so that the judgements gave each other mutual support. In such a case, favourable reasons could be known to exist for the truth of any judgement, and yet such reasons might not be specified. Further, it could be known that there was a potential infinity of such reasons, without it being the case that it had to be possible for such judgements to be specified.

For example, suppose that the truth of 'a' is a reason for the truth of 'b', and that the truth of 'b' is a reason for the truth of 'c', and that the truth of 'c' is a reason for the truth of 'a'. The judgement that b could be supported by the judgement that a. A reason for the truth of this judgement would be the judgement that c, a reason for the truth of that judgement would be the judgement that b, and a reason for the truth of that judgement would be the judgement that a. It is obvious in such a situation that reasons could be given as far as was ever desired. A protagonist who made the first few judgements would be perfectly justified in thinking that favourable reasons existed, however far they might be pursued. Yet he might not, perhaps could not, make more than the first few judgements. Here favourable reasons would be known to exist, and a potentially infinite number of them at that, without their being specified, and even if it was impossible to specify them all. It seems, therefore, as if it might be possible for an atemporal world to satisfy the first premiss since, in an analogous way, its protagonist might know that there were a potentially infinite number of favourable reasons without being able to specify them. Here reasons would be available enabling him to distinguish between his true and his false judgements, and also reasons for those reasons, without it being the case that he would have to specify all those reasons and so possess an infinite intellect.

This is not to deny that the formal feature that the protagonist could know in that world more than he does know in that world could not be contained in an atemporal world. It is simply to deny that various arguments which were meant to show that this formal feature is part of any comprehensible world really do so. These arguments purported to show that only worlds which possessed this feature would satisfy the first premiss without requiring that the protagonist be in possession of an actual infinity of reasons, and so have an infinite intellect. However, it has just been seen that they do not show this since it has been demonstrated that the first premiss would be satisfied in a world which did not contain the feature in question. For it is possible for a protagonist to know that a potentially infinite number of reasons support the judgements that he makes without ever having to, or even being able to, specify them all. At least so far, then, it has not been demonstrated that an atemporal world is also an incomprehensible one.

§25   THAT JUSTIFICATION HAS AN END

There is another objection to the argument that was attempted at the beginning of the last section which is worth discussing for its own sake and for the light that it throws on any comprehensible world. The first move in the argument depended on giving the first premiss of this inquiry unrestricted scope so that any reason that the protagonist produced or could produce for a judgement was itself regarded as a further judgement which needed reasons for its support. It might be objected to this that, although reasons must be available for the truth or falsity of some judgements, and that some reasons can be given for these reasons, these reasons form a finite chain which has an end in judgements which do not need further justification.

If this familiar objection is to be of immediate interest to this inquiry, it must not just be made as an attempt to describe what actually goes on in our own world, but rather as an attempt to assert a formal feature of justification as such. If it is to be an objection, that is, it must assert that there is something about all use of justifications or reasons as such that prevents the first premiss of this inquiry applying with unrestricted scope. The objection, for example, seems to have this general, or formal, nature in Wittgenstein when he remarks that 'Justification by experience comes to an end. If it did not it would not be justification' (*Invest.*, §485). It is convenient in any case to examine this objection with reference to Wittgenstein since, as pointed out in §16, he also uses a principle of argument almost exactly similar to the first premiss. It is to be expected, therefore, that it is possible to find not only a development of the present objection in Wittgenstein but also a way of reconciling it with the first premiss.

It might, however, be thought that when Wittgenstein asserted that justification had an end, he was not remarking on a formal feature of justification as such but merely describing what we actually do in this world. It is certainly true that sometimes when he is making remarks analogous to this one he is merely concerned with pointing out the facts about how we at present carry on. An example of this is: 'When someone whom I am afraid of orders me to continue the series, I act quickly, with perfect certainty, and the lack of reasons does not trouble me' (*Invest.*, §212). At times Wittgenstein's interest is merely to point out that we do not actually think of a reason before we decide, or that we could not go through all the reasons before we decide. An example of this is: 'There need not have been a reason for the choice. A reason is a step preceding the step of the choice. But why should every step be preceded by another one?' (*Brown Book*, p. 88). This failure to think of the reasons before deciding does not mean that reasons could not be available for deciding the truth or falsity of the judgement in question, as Wittgenstein himself points out on another occasion: 'The question: "On what grounds do you believe this?" might mean: "From what you are now deducing it (have you just deduced it)?" But it might also mean: "What grounds can you produce for this assumption on thinking it over?"' (*Invest.*, §479). So it is best to take Wittgenstein's remarks about how we do not actually go through the reasons before we judge as just describing a fact about our present practice rather than as indicating a formal property of reasons as such.

However, certain other of Wittgenstein's remarks about justification coming to an end do intend to point out a formal feature of justification as such, rather than merely describing what we at present do. These remarks indicate not just that we need not go further along the chain of reasons than we do, but that the chain of reasons itself comes to an end. They indicate, that is, not just that we use a finite number of reasons in practice, with others being available, but that we must use such a finite number because a point comes at which no more reasons are available. Such remarks are: 'If I have exhausted the justifications I have reached bedrock, and my spade is turned' (*Invest.*, §217), or: 'You will be at a loss to answer this question, and find that here we strike rock bottom, that is we have come down to the conventions' (*Blue Book*, p. 24). These remarks indicate not just that there are reasons available which are not actually used, but that the reasons themselves come to an end, and that a point is reached at which none are available even if they are wanted.

Wittgenstein, therefore, is certainly at times pointing to a formal feature of justification as such in his remarks about justification coming to an end. He also provides a way of understanding why there should be such a formal property. This is by showing that rules could not always be provided which specified how other rules were to be applied and that, therefore, some rules must be applied without the use of further rules. He illustrates this neatly in the *Blue Book* when he discusses which way an arrow means us to go. He wonders if the way could be indicated by placing a second arrow under the first and continues:

Suppose we write down the scheme of saying and meaning by a column of arrows one below the other.

Then if this scheme is to serve our purpose at all, it must show us which of the three levels is the level of meaning. I can, e.g., make a scheme with three levels, the bottom level always being the level of meaning. But adopt whatever model or scheme you may, it will have a bottom level, and there will be no such thing as an interpretation of that. To say in this case that every arrow can still be interpreted would only mean that I *could* always make a different model of saying and meaning which had one more level than the one I am using (*Blue Book*, p. 34).

This argument appears in condensed form in the *Investigations* where it appears, for example, in the following remark: ' "The line intimates to me which way I am to go" is only a paraphrase of: it is my *last* arbiter for the way I am to go' (§230).

That justification has an end appeared to be an objection to, or at least a severe modification of, the first premiss of the present inquiry. This is understandable if it is taken in the formal way just illustrated, for a judgement without reasons being available with which to decide its truth or falsity is, according to the first premiss, idle in comprehension of a world. Yet if the doctrine that justification comes to an end is correct, then there must be many such judgements for which no reasons are available. At the point at which reasons come to an end, that is, the judgements made would be perfectly idle. Yet if the chain of reasons ends in idle judgements, there seems no way of preventing this idleness from spreading up the chain. On the other hand, if idleness in judgements is prevented by giving full scope to the first premiss and allowing that further reasons may always be available, then it seems that this would involve justification having no end. So it seems impossible to support simultaneously the doctrine that justification comes to an end and the doctrine embodied in the first premiss. For if the first doctrine is held, it seems that there can be no reasons available in the way that the first premiss requires. On the other hand, if the doctrine expressed in the first premiss is given full scope, it seems that reasons cannot come to an end.

Wittgenstein, however, seems to give support to both these doctrines, and so it is to be expected that he also uses some way of dividing their spheres of influence so that they do not prevent each other's operation in the way that they appear to do when each is given unrestricted scope. A clue to how he does this may be found in the cases Wittgenstein examines in detail to show how justification comes to an end, such as the one quoted at length above. These cases aim at demonstrating that there cannot always be a rule which lays down how we are to follow another rule; that there cannot be an infinite hierarchy of rules. Wittgenstein thinks that this applies particularly for the rules that might be given for the application of the same word to the same kind of thing.

With regard to the application of the same word to the same kind of thing, there does not seem to be much hope of dividing the spheres of influence of the two doctrines. For this is obviously a clear case of an area in which the doctrine embodied in the first premiss has application, and so one which cannot be reserved for the application of the doctrine that justification comes to an end. However, Wittgenstein's example of rules being used for the application of other rules need not only be applied to the question of whether the correct terms are being used. For it is possible to arrange the laws of a world in a hierarchy of laws about laws, and it is possible to regard all these laws as rules which have to be followed if correct judgements are to be made. So a possible application of Wittgenstein's argument is that such hierarchies of laws, or rules, must also be finite.

In the example of Wittgenstein's quoted at length above, that is, the rules lay down what other rules apply and when they apply. In a world which contains a hierarchy of laws there is a similar situation; some laws lay down which other laws apply and when they apply. Wittgenstein argues that the former hierarchy, at least in some cases, is a finite one. It seems reasonable to suppose that the latter hierarchy is also a finite one, and that it is impossible to keep on giving laws about what other laws are to apply in various situations. In particular, it seems reasonable to suppose that such a hierarchy of laws comes to an end at the point in which there is a law which says that laws may be operated in the world in question. Such a law is sometimes called the principle of the uniformity of nature and the problem of its justification is the familiar problem of the justification of induction. A natural and familiar line to take with this problem is to take induction as the point at which justification comes to an end. This, for example, is the line taken by Strawson who says about reasoning inductively that 'Doing this is what "being reasonable" *means* in such a context' (*Introduction to Logical Theory*, p. 257). It is also the line taken by Wittgenstein four sections before his claim that justification by experience comes to an end: 'If anyone said that information about the past could not convince him that something would happen in the future, I should not understand him. One might ask him: . . . if *these* are not grounds, then what are grounds?' (*Invest.*, §481).

It does seem reasonable, therefore, to presume that Wittgenstein held that the hierarchy of laws is finite. For unless Wittgenstein held such a principle (or at least the more limited one relating to the application of terms), then he would have no way of making a division between the spheres of operation of the two requirements that he uses at different times in argument, the requirement that justification comes to an end and the requirement that there must be criteria of correctness with which to distinguish between what is correct and what merely seems to be so.

If this is the way that the doctrine that justification has an end is taken, then this shows that it need not lead to a severe modification of the first premiss, even if it is considered to be a correct doctrine. For it would still allow the derivation from the first premiss with which this chapter began, namely that there is a potential infinity of reasons available to the protagonist enabling him to distinguish between his true judgements and his false judgements. For even if there is a limitation on the rules that can be given for the correct use of terms, and even if there is a finite hierarchy of laws, this does not mean that a particular judgement and a particular law may not have an infinite number of reasons available for its support. In the particular model worlds considered in the last chapter, for example, in which the world was taken to pass through a succession of states which kept repeating the same pattern, a potentially infinite number of judgements was available to support any particular judgement even though there were only a few simple laws, and these laws were of the same level.

The purpose of this section is to show that even if the doctrine that justification comes to an end is accepted, it does not spoil the argument of the first part of the chapter which showed that the first premiss involved a potentially infinite number of reasons being available to the protagonist of a comprehensible world. It might also be doubted whether the doctrine itself is sound, at least in its stronger form. For although in any series of rules as given or as written out in the kind of scheme of arrows used in the long quotation above there will always be a last line, this does not necessarily mean that there need be a last reason or a last arrow when these reasons or arrows are thought of as merely potential, as merely being available if required.

The first part of the argument of §24 can be upheld, then, even if it is thought to be the case that justification has an end. This, however, does not avoid the difficulties in the argument that were found in the second part of that section. For it still remains the case that even if a potentially infinite number of reasons have to be available to the protagonist he might know that such reasons were available without specifying them all. So, as argued in the last section, it still remains to be shown that an atemporal world is an incomprehensible one.

§26 THAT THE MAJORITY OF JUDGEMENTS ARE CORRECT

It was remarked near the end of the last section that even if there were a finite hierarchy of laws there could still be a potentially infinite number of reasons available for the truth or falsity of any particular judgement. For in the particular model worlds which continually changed their states, there might be a potentially infinite number of judgements of subsequent states which could be used to support the judgement of one particular state. This, however, is not a way of satisfying the first premiss and the requirement that justification comes to an end (if this is felt to be a sound requirement) which would be available in an atemporal world unless it is also assumed that it is possible for a protagonist to have an infinitely large intellect. For, since such a protagonist would have to make all his judgements (as we on the outside would say) simultaneously, he would have to make an infinite number of judgements if this situation is to be reproduced in an atemporal world.

It will be remembered that the example that was given of a situation in which an infinite number of reasons might be known to be available without their being specified was that of a circle of reasons. There could be such a circle between several particular judgements and the judgement of a law that is being used to support them. Here, for example, the judgements 'x', 'y', and 'z' could be used to support the law 'always y between x and z' and the law 'always y between x and z' could be used to support the judgements 'x', 'y', and 'z'. It is obvious that such justification could be continued as far as desired, and it is obvious that it can be known that there are a potentially infinite number of reasons available without their all being specified. If, therefore, the kind of potential infinity of reasons required by the first premiss is only of this kind, it will be easy to satisfy in an atemporal world. If, however, an infinity of reasons which cannot be given by such a circle in justification is required, then it will not be possible for an atemporal world to satisfy the first premiss unless it is also allowed to be possible that there could be a protagonist with an intellect of infinite capacity.

In this section an attempt will be made to argue that the first premiss requires this stronger kind of infinity of reasons and cannot merely be satisfied with a circle in justification. If this can be shown, it will mean that a comprehensible atemporal world is only possible if an infinite intellect is possible. It will, at least, form a strong inclining argument for the necessity of time in any comprehensible world, if not an absolutely conclusive one. This stronger kind of infinity of reasons will have been demonstrated if it can be shown that in any comprehensible world there has to be a potentially infinite number of particular judgements. So to show that an atemporal world would be an incomprehensible one, it must be shown that it must always be possible to produce further particular judgements whenever the laws or other particular judgements need to be supported.

Laws were found to be needed in §18 when it was realized that only if there were general principles of connection between judgements would a protagonist be able to distinguish between his true and his false judgements. In §23 it was seen that these laws would themselves need support; and the argument of §25 suggested that this support could not come from all the judgements being placed in a hierarchy and all being supported or justified by some master-law at the top. It seems, therefore, as if a circle of support is required between the laws and the instances. This may not be the only way in which the requirements of the first premiss can be satisfied, but it is the most obvious way. In this circle, or interdependence, of justification, the judgements of the instances must not always be preferred to the law (as was seen in §18) and yet the law must be supported by the instances. The present question is whether an open set, or potentially infinite number, of instances is required for this; or whether such support might not be provided by a closed set, or specifiably finite number, of instances.

This feature that the world must be arranged in a law-like manner is obviously only a necessary condition of a world being a comprehensible one. It is not in itself sufficient. It will not enable the protagonist of a world to isolate particular judgements as true or false unless he employs another method in addition to laws to tell him about the truth of his judgements. For all that the laws can tell him by themselves is that if certain of his judgements are true then certain other judgements of his are false. Unless, however, he knows which judgements are true, he cannot use this knowledge to determine with the help of the laws the truth or falsity of others of his judgements. The laws enable him to decide which of the judgements he does or could make are incompatible with one another. They do not enable him to tell which member of an incompatible pair is true and which member is false. It is clear that he can do this only if he can rely on some further assumption which enables him to isolate particular judgements as being true or false without use of the laws.

Some other feature in addition to the use of laws is required, therefore, if the protagonist is to be able to distinguish between those judgements of his which are true and those judgements of his which are false. This feature will be another way of isolating certain judgements as being true. Obviously it can only do this either in virtue of the content of those particular judgements or in virtue of the relation that they bear to all other judgements. They must be regarded as true, that is, either because of their subject-matter or because of the particular position that they occupy in the system of judgements as a whole. There seems to be no obvious subject-matter of judgements that would perform this function. Isolating a set of judgements as being true just because they are about a certain subject-matter seems just the kind of thing that needs support in accordance with the demands of the first premiss, and so cannot be used as an independent starting-point for the kind of justification that the first premiss requires. Isolating a particular set of judgements as correct because of the relation that they bear to other judgements and because of the particular position that this set of judgements occupies in the structure of judgements as a whole does not seem to be objectionable in this way. So the additional means of isolating true judgements to the use of laws is one that should involve the use of the position of certain judgements in the structure of the protagonist's judgements as a whole rather than the use of the content of certain judgements.

Such a feature, relating to the structural position rather than to the content of judgements, is that the protagonist must take the majority of his direct judgements about the world as being correct. A protagonist, that is, can distinguish between true judgements and false judgements in the way required by the first premiss if he is allowed to assume in addition that the majority of the direct judgements that he makes are true (or, of any judgement, that it may be taken to be true unless shown to be false). This means was covertly used, for example, in §17 when apparent memories of going up Whitehall and of seeing the Arc de Triomphe were discussed. It is true that, as was asserted there, the several apparent memories about going up Whitehall are reasons for the falsity of the apparent memory about seeing the Arc de Triomphe. However, it is also true that the single memory about the Arc de Triomphe is a reason for the falsity of all the apparent memories about going up Whitehall. If, therefore, someone is going to be able to distinguish between the truth and falsity of all these apparent memories, some independent means must be available, enabling him to decide between the possibility that the London memories are true and the Paris memory false and the possibility that the Paris memory is true and the London memories false. For all the laws of the present world will tell him is that they cannot both be true. It would seem intolerably arbitrary, and would also conflict with the first premiss of the present inquiry, if this independent means depended upon the content of the judgement in question so that, for example, all judgements about London were always taken as true and all judgements about Paris taken as false. On the contrary, the natural method to use, and the one used without comment when this example was discussed above, is that of taking the largest set of judgements that fits coherently together (fits together in accordance with the laws) as correct. This is why the apparent memories of Whitehall could be taken to support each other's truth, and taken as isolating the apparent memory of the Arc de Triomphe as a false one.

It appears, therefore, that another feature which is required if a world is to be comprehensible to its protagonist is that he take the majority of his direct judgements about that world, or the largest coherent set of his judgements, as being correct. This conclusion is put somewhat tentatively since, whereas it is clear that something more is required than the use of laws if judgements are to be isolated as being true or false, it has not been demonstrated that there is no alternative means of doing this to taking the majority of direct judgements as being correct; and unless, of course, it is demonstrated that no alternative method will serve, it will not have been shown that this feature is an essential one in any comprehensible world. However, it can be assumed that even if this precise feature is not essential, then something like it must be. This gives enough for the succeeding argument, in which it is examined whether such a feature could be possessed by an atemporal world.

The superiority of taking the majority of direct judgements as being correct (or of some other feature like it) as a means of distinguishing which judgements were correct, depended upon the fact that this did not involve specifying any particular judgements as being correct. It was merely another formal feature discovered to be essential in any comprehensible world, and so one which would be satisfied in different particular worlds in different ways and by different kinds of judgements. It provides, that is, a way in which the laws of a particular world may be operated so that true judgements can be achieved, but does not itself prescribe what the specific true judgements are. In an atemporal world, however, with a known and finite set of judgements (assuming an infinitely large intellect is impossible), this feature of assuming that the majority of judgements are correct will prescribe what the actual correct judgements are. For example, in a world with five judgements made by the protagonist, v, w, x, y, z, which are so linked together by the laws that the truth of v, w, x, and y is incompatible with the truth of z, to take the majority of judgements as correct just is to take v, w, x, and y as correct. It is to specify, that is, that certain particular judgements are correct. The situation is very different from this in a temporal world in which the truth of all the judgements made in one world is not known at one time or in a world with a poten-

tially infinite number of judgements. For in such worlds adoption of the feature that the majority of judgements are correct
does not involve specifying any particular judgements as being
correct; whatever judgements form part of the majority of
judgements at one time, it is always possible that these judgements will not be part of the majority at another time.

At first sight, therefore, it seems that an important distinction which can be made in a temporal world could not be
made in an atemporal one. For the whole point of taking the
majority of judgements as correct as an independent means
of isolating true judgements was that it was a method which
relied upon the judgements' over-all structure rather than on
their specific content, and so a method which did not fall foul
of the first premiss. However, this distinction seems to be
blurred in the case of an atemporal world, for here to take the
majority of judgements as correct is just to take a certain specific set of judgements as correct. This could be put forward
as an argument designed to show that an atemporal world
was impossible if it was also to be a comprehensible one.

On further reflection, however, it is clear that this argument will not work. For although the requirement that the
majority of judgements be taken as correct does lead in the
atemporal world to the taking of a certain particular set of
judgements as correct, nevertheless the reason that this particular set of judgements is taken as correct is a reason based on
structure rather than content. This particular set has been
isolated as correct because it is the largest coherent set of
judgements, and not because these judgements have a particular content or subject-matter. The only difference between
an atemporal world and a temporal one is that the consequence of this structural requirement can be drawn immediately and certainly rather than subsequently and tentatively.
This can give the impression that the requirement has ceased
to be part of the structure of justification in an atemporal
world and has been replaced by something more substantial,
more connected with the content of the judgements. This,
however, would be a mistaken impression: these particular
judgements are taken as correct not because of anything to do
with their subject-matter but because they form the largest
coherent set of judgements in that world. Although, therefore, interesting further features of any comprehensible world

have emerged in this section, these features are features which an atemporal world could possess and so do not show an atemporal world to be an incomprehensible one.

§27 ATEMPORAL AND TEMPORAL WORLDS

In this chapter an attempt has been made to show that an atemporal world could not be a comprehensible one. This attempt has not been successful. The attempt was also made in order to discover further features of the general model world at this most primitive level; and also to show how it is possible to think on both sides of the limit of comprehensibility by showing how it is possible to argue about whether something as deeply seated in our present conceptual scheme as time is an essential feature of any world which we could understand. This has been relatively successful. A picture has also been given of how different an atemporal world would be from our present one. This can be used as the basis of an inclining argument in favour of the introduction of time as an essential feature of any comprehensible world, even if this cannot be demonstrated absolutely.

The different ways in which the feature that the majority of judgements should be taken as correct can be satisfied in a temporal and an atemporal world shows how different the two kinds of world are and how much more easily the first premiss may be satisfied in a temporal world. Just as it is possible that in a temporal world, the set of judgements that form the majority of judgements may change in composition, so also is it always possible that further, and independent, reasons for any judgement may turn up. The set of judgements that are made in an atemporal world must be taken as constituting the protagonist's knowledge of that world. However, if the same set of judgements were made in a temporal world it would always be possible for further judgements to be made which would show that all these judgements were quite false. By the same token, further judgements could be made which would serve as independent reasons for their truth. Better and more independent reasons are therefore available to the protagonist of a temporal world attempting to distinguish between his true judgements and his false ones. So a temporal world satisfies the requirement of the first premiss better than an atemporal one does.

The difference between the two kinds of worlds that this argument brings out can be seen by comparing two model worlds, one of which has a finite number of instances of its laws (and so a finite number of judgements about those instances) and the other of which has an indefinitely large number of such instances, not all of which are at any one time judged by its protagonist. The latter of these two particular model worlds obviously satisfies the first premiss better than the former one does. For, although an indefinite number of reasons is available for the truth of the judgements in the first model world (because of possibilities of circles in justification between judgements of the instances and judgements of the laws), the mechanism for setting up such an indefinitely large chain of specified reasons is logically secondary to the judgements of the instances themselves. These reasons, that is, can never lead to an alteration in one of the initial judgements of the instances. In the second particular model world, by contrast, the reasons which could be produced may easily lead to an alteration of judgements that have already been made. They are not, therefore, logically secondary to the initial judgements of the instances but independent and powerful reasons. In both the two particular model worlds, that is, a potential infinity of reasons is available with which particular judgements of instances may be supported. However, in the first particular model world these reasons are not really independent and cannot provide the kind of support that the second set of reasons can. This is why the second of these two particular model worlds satisfies the first premiss better and in a fuller way than the first one does.

It is clear, therefore, that a temporal world satisfies the first premiss better than an atemporal one does. This cannot be an absolutely conclusive argument that time is essential in any comprehensible world; but it can be an inclining argument in favour of the assumption of time as essential as a new premiss in the inquiry. It will be remembered that in §21 it was shown that either time or space was essential in any comprehensible world. Since it is generally agreed that time is more fundamental than space in the comprehension of a world, the safest way to use this result if neither can be shown independently to be essential is to assume that time is. For these reasons, or just as a further acceptable premiss of the inquiry it will be assumed in future that time is an essential feature of any comprehensible world.

§28 STATE OF THE INQUIRY

The general inquiry is into the essential conditions of any world being a comprehensible one. This was visualized in §10 as the construction of what is being called the general model world. At its inmost level of austerity or necessity some feature or features would be assumed which were absolutely essential in any comprehensible world. The preconditions of this feature or features would then be examined to see what other features were essential at this inmost level of necessity. When no more features could be derived at this level, recourse was to be had to a second premiss by means of which a further feature or features could be introduced and the argument start again. Such an additional premiss would move the conclusions to a second, and lesser, level of austerity or necessity.

This programme has been followed in the last two chapters. An extremely fundamental feature was presumed by the first premiss of the inquiry, introduced in §15. The other features required by this feature were then argued for, and various conclusions about them were established in §§17 and 18 of the last chapter and §§21, 25, and 26 of this chapter. This built up a picture of the inmost level of the general model world. It was attempted, also, to derive time as another feature of the general model world at this inmost level. This, however, was unsuccessful and although good inclining arguments could be found for the introduction of time it could not be shown to follow conclusively from the other features that have already been demonstrated. Accordingly, it was decided at the end of the last section to adopt a second premiss and assume that time was an essential feature of any comprehensible world. With the adoption of such a second premiss the inquiry now moves to its second level of necessity or austerity.

The general model world, therefore, has now moved to the layer in which time is added to the original premiss. This has obvious consequences for any particular model worlds developed to represent features of the general model world at this level. In such worlds, for example, it would be possible for the protagonist to change his mind about certain judgements, to hold certain judgements to be true for a while and then judge them to be false. It will be the case that the protagonist of such a world, that is, could know more than he does know in that world. It is now possible for worlds to satisfy the first premiss by the simple device of allowing them to contain a potential infinity of reasons, as many of which can be elicited as is ever desired. It is true, of course, that an atemporal world could contain a potential infinity of reasons, but these reasons, unspecified and created by a formula, could not have the independent force or surprise effect of the individual members of a potentially infinite chain of reasons in a temporal world. As described in the last section, only in a temporal world could these reasons be sufficiently strong and independent to lead to the withdrawal of a judgement already made.

In a temporal world, therefore, it is always possible that the judgements taken to be correct at one time should subsequently be found to be false. Conversely, it is always possible in a temporal world to find further and independent support for the judgements that are true. The laws of a temporal world are likewise open to testing, open to confirmation or falsification. One immediate consequence of the new premiss, therefore, is that it is always possible that the judgements which form the largest set of coherent judgements at one time should subsequently be shown to be false. Similarly, it is always possible that mistakes should be found in the laws that a model world is held to fulfil. These consequences could be expressed by saying that the general model world with time also contains testing, since the laws that are held to apply at any one time will be tested by subsequent judgements and might be found not to apply.

The general model world with time, therefore, also contains testing. This testing, however, is what could be called static testing; it is merely an indication that what are taken to be the laws of a model world are always open to revision in the light of future experience. The general model world with time does not necessarily contain what could be called active testing; it has not been shown or assumed, that is, that the protagonist can interfere with his world in order to test any laws that he might feel in doubt about. If this is an essential feature of the general model world at this level, it will have to be shown to be such.

CHAPTER FIVE

Perception

§29 INTRODUCTION

THE next question to be considered is whether the general model world at its present second level of necessity or austerity contains some feature which means that it is impossible for a world just of sensations to be a comprehensible one. This question is obviously of central importance to many theories and worries about perception. It relates directly to such theories as phenomenalism or idealism when these theories are set up in an ontological way; when they assert, that is, that nothing really exists except sensations or perceptions. If it can be shown that the objects of the judgements made in any particular model world which represents the general model world at this level can not be taken to be the sensations of its protagonist, then these theories will have been found to be false. It will have been shown, that is, that they could not apply to any comprehensible world, and so could not apply to our own present world.

If these theories are found to be false, then the alternative language theory (the theory that a sensation language and a material object language are complete but independent ways of describing the present world), in most of its forms, will also have been found to be false. For since this theory holds that a sensation language really is a complete and independent way of describing the phenomena, then, if it were correct, it would follow that the world would be just the same if nothing did in fact exist except sensations. The alternative language theory, that is, must contain as part of itself the claim that it is possible to have a world which just contains sensations and yet which is as complex as the present one. If, therefore, it can be shown that the objects of any comprehensible world, and so the objects of the present world, cannot all be taken to be sensations, then it will have been shown that this claim, and so all normal versions of the alternative language theory, is false.

The method which will be used to examine whether there could be a comprehensible world consisting just of sensations is similar to the method used to examine whether an atemporal world was comprehensible. First some feature must be found which would be impossible in any world consisting just of sensations. Then an attempt must be made to see whether this feature follows from the features that have already been derived in the construction of the general model world. If this can be accomplished, it will have been shown that a world consisting just of sensations could not be a comprehensible one.

First, therefore, a feature must be found which could not be possessed by a world consisting just of sensations, and which there is a reasonable chance of being able to derive in the present situation of the general model world. Features which refer either to the structure or else to the truth of the protagonist's judgements are likely to be most suitable. Yet, naturally enough, the features which most obviously could not be possessed by a world consisting just of sensations relate to the possibilities of certain kinds of perception rather than to the possibilities of certain kinds of judgement. For example, it is obvious that a world consisting just of sensations could not possess the feature that the same objects of perception exist unperceived between occasions of perception. This is a feature relating to sensation, and which does not look as if it has a direct replacement in terms of judgement. However, suppose that we understand by 'direct judgement' judgement without inference of the present situation. Then it might be thought that perception could be simply replaced by direct judgement, so that conditions on the objects of perception were equivalent to conditions on the objects of direct judgement. If this substitution is permissible, then the possibility of objects existing unperceived (which is a feature which obviously could not be possessed by a world consisting just of sensations) would be equivalent to, and could be replaced by, the possibility of objects existing without being directly judged (which is a feature which may well be derivable in the present state of the general model world). So if it is permissible to treat perception and direct judgement as being equivalent, then the possibility of objects existing without being directly judged is the sought after feature.

In the way that direct judgement has been handled in the model worlds discussed so far it seems fair enough to assume that occasions of direct judgement are occasions of perception. Perceptual judgements obviously form a sub-class of judgements made immediately about a world; and it would seem to be quite permissible to take them as comprising the whole class, so that every direct judgement was considered to be a perceptual judgement. In a world in which direct judgements were made about objects quite different from those in the present world, that is, it would be quite natural to say that the people in that world could perceive differently. If someone, for example, could judge directly and non-inferentially how the objects were in the next room, then it would be quite natural to say that they were possessed of some mysterious perceptual faculty which enabled them to perceive the next room. It seems quite possible, therefore, to take all occasions of direct judgement as being occasions of perception.

If, however, it is permissible to replace perception by direct judgement, so that all conditions on direct judgement are conditions on perception, it must not only be the case that every occasion of direct judgement is an occasion of perception but also be the case that every occasion of perception is an occasion of direct judgement. Consider, for example, the proposal to replace the possibility of existence unperceived with the possibility of existence unjudged. Unless it is the case that every occasion of perception is an occasion of direct judgement so that, for any object, its perception implies its direct judgement, the absence of direct judgement will not show the absence of perception, and the possibility of existence unjudged will not entail the possibility of existence unperceived. So for this replacement of perception by direct judgement to be permissible, it must not only be permissible to take every occasion of direct judgement as an occasion of perception but also permissible to take every occasion of perception as an occasion of direct judgement.

It seems possible, however, to have cases of perception which are not cases of direct judgement. It seems, for example, that I can properly be said to see things in this world which I do not pay any attention to nor form any judgements about. Perhaps a suitably extended sense of 'judgement' can be used so that these are all cases of judgement. Yet in the narrow sense of 'judgement' in which it just covers some verbal or quasi-verbal report I make to myself or others, there are obviously many things which I see, but about which I make no judgement. In this narrower sense of 'judgement' I obviously do not judge that I have a sensation all the time that I have it. For example, I might have a headache all the morning. Yet I might only judge that I have it at 9 a.m. and 11 a.m. In between I perceive it without judging it. So perception does not imply judgement, and the absence of judgement does not imply the absence of perception. In this case, that is, the headache exists unjudged but it does not exist unperceived. So as long as 'judgement' is understood in this narrow way, conditions on perception cannot be replaced by conditions on judgement, and demonstrating the possibility of existence unjudged would not show the possibility of existence unperceived.

Unless 'judgement' is understood in a rather wide sense, therefore, it is not possible to replace conditions on perception by conditions on judgement, and the feature that it must be possible for objects to exist unjudged is not one which obviously could not be possessed by a world just of sensations. In these circumstances it seems best not to argue for this feature if it is possible to find some alternative which does not depend upon specifying special senses of 'judgement'. There does not seem to be any obvious candidate for this, but there is one feature which involves no special sense of 'judgement' and has been repeatedly taken to be a feature which is not possessed by a world consisting just of sensations. This is the feature that it is possible that the protagonist should be in error in some of his judgements about the present state of the world. Although it is not obvious that this feature could not be possessed by a world consisting just of sensations, those philosophers who have adopted a phenomenalist basis to their systems by taking as their basic objects sense data or ideas have thought that these objects possessed two fundamental characteristics, that they could not exist unperceived and that their experiencer could not be in error in present tense judgements about them. If it can be shown that it is a feature of the general model world that it must be possible that the protagonist should be in error in some of his present tense judgements, then it will have been shown that no comprehensible world can possess basic objects having the second of these two characteristics. This will, at the very least, form an argument against the phenomenalists, and it would be natural to expect that it might form the basis of an argument showing that no comprehensible world can possess basic objects having the first of these two characteristics. Historically, that is, these two characteristics have been thought to go together. It is natural to suppose, therefore, that an argument against one of them should form the basis of an argument against the other of them.

In any case, an attempt will be made in the following section to derive the feature that it must be possible for the protagonist to be in error in some of his present tense judgements about the world. It is hoped that establishing this feature will form an intermediate step in the derivation of the impossibility of a world consisting just of sensations, and so this feature will be dubbed the intermediate feature. Even if this hope is unfulfilled, the important role that its contradictory (the feature that it is not possible for the protagonist to be mistaken in present tense judgements) has played in phenomenalist accounts means that establishing it will be an important step in any critique of phenomenalism. It might, indeed, be said that the characteristic mark of phenomenalism was that it removed the possibility of error from direct present tense judgements about the objects of the world and replaced it by the possibility of error in judgements about the relations between objects. On a phenomenalist account, if I make a mistake, this is a mistake in the objects that I predict I shall be confronted with or a mistake in the objects that I remember having been confronted with. It is not a mistake about the object that I am at present confronted with. For example, my mistake with regard to the stick in the water is in thinking that it will look straight when it comes out of the water (when I have a stick-like sense datum without a water-like sense datum). This is a mistake in anticipation; and it is not held that I make any direct mistakes about what the stick is like at the time that I perceive it. If, therefore, it can be shown that it must be possible for the protagonist to be in error in some of his present tense judgements about the world, this basic tenet of phenomenalism will have been shown to be inapplicable in any comprehensible world.

§30 ARGUMENT FOR THE INTERMEDIATE FEATURE

The aim of this section is to see whether the feature that it must be possible for the protagonist to be in error in some of the judgements he makes about his present situation follows directly from the other features that have already been derived. It was discovered in §18 that a feature of any comprehensible world was that its protagonist must be prepared on some occasions to follow what the laws of the world described the situation as, rather than what he would otherwise have judged it to be. The protagonist, that is, must be prepared to allow that some of his immediate judgements about how the world is could be mistaken. Time has now been assumed to be a feature of any comprehensible world, and so the question arises of how the result of §18 is to be interpreted. For it can be asked whether this general result, that the protagonist must be prepared to think of at least some of his judgements being wrong, applies also to a subset of his judgements that can be isolated by means of time, whether, that is, the protagonist must also be prepared to think that some of his judgements about his present situation could be mistaken. This is the question considered in the present section, for if the general result does apply to that subset then the intermediate feature will have been shown to follow from the features that have already been derived.

Judgements that the protagonist makes about his present situation may be called present judgements. Present judgements are judgements in which the time at which the state of affairs being judged is supposed to obtain is the same time as the time at which the judgement is made. Judgements which are not present judgements, then, are judgements made at different times from the time at which the state of affairs judged is supposed to obtain. Someone, such as a phenomenalist, who wishes to show that the intermediate feature does not follow from the other features already derived must show, therefore, that these latter judgements are the only judgements in which the possibility of error required by §18 can arise.

A phenomenalist would be liable to describe these other judgements as predictions and memory judgements. So if he wishes to block the argument to the intermediate feature he must show that the possibility of error required by §18 need only arise for predictions and memory judgements. Such a result would in any case be in accord with the phenomenalist policy mentioned in the last section of allowing error to arise in the connections between judgements rather than in the straightforward judgements about how the world actually is. For errors in memory judgements could be taken as errors in judgements about what the present judgements made some time ago actually were, and errors in predictions could be taken as errors in judgements about what the future present judgements will be. Memories and predictions, that is, are just judgements made now about what other present judgements were or will be; on the phenomenalist policy these are the only ones in which mistake is allowed. There can be no question of mistake in the present judgements which form the foundation of the whole system.

Now this phenomenalist policy has to be shown to be mistaken if the necessity of the intermediate feature is to be demonstrated. As mentioned above, argument for such a policy must depend on showing that the general principle of the possibility of error in judgements, which was demonstrated in §18, does not apply to all judgements but only to some. This principle arose in §18 because it was realized that any law which can be used to distinguish between truth and falsity must be such that judgements based on it could be preferred by the protagonist to his immediate judgement of instances. In any major field of the protagonist's judgements, therefore, he must be able to prefer the law to the immediate judgement of the instances, and so must be able to consider some of his immediate judgements about that field to be false. The principle of the possibility of error, therefore, applies to all major fields of the protagonist's judgements. The only way, therefore, in which an area of judgements can be shown to be one to which the principle does not apply is if it can be shown to be a less important area of judgement which is secondary to, and dependent upon, such a major area. So a defender of the phenomenalist policy must show that present judgements are of secondary importance in our judgements about the world.

A defender of the phenomenalist policy might, accordingly, attempt to argue that only a minority of the judgements that we at present make are present judgements. Someone, for example, describing his entire situation at one time will normally rely on more memory judgements than present ones. Indeed, it might be urged, it would be possible for someone to make very complex judgements about how his world was and had been, solving problems about incompatibilities between various of his judgements in order to do so, at a time in which none of the judgements that he was making were present judgements at all (as such a term would be understood by a phenomenalist; judgements about those parts of the world that could not at that time be seen would, properly speaking, be predictions or conditional judgements).

Such an argument for the phenomenalist policy, however, will not work. It depends on evaluating the status of present judgements in incompatible ways. It is important for the argument just made, and for any argument that seeks to exempt present judgements from the scope of the principle of the possibility of error, that present judgements should be seen to play a minor and unimportant part in the protagonist's thought about his world. Yet this is just the role that present judgements cannot play in the phenomenalist policy, for it is an important part of this policy that present judgements are at the foundation of the system and that other judgements are only about what present judgements were made or will be made. In other words, there is a trick in the argument urged in favour of the phenomenalist policy that present judgements formed only a tiny part of the totality of judgements taken into consideration while forming a complex decision about the nature of the world, or even that there might be some cases in which no present judgements were used. For this argument ignored the fact that, according to the phenomenalist policy, the memory judgements that were used instead were themselves based on present judgements, only ones made at other times. Thus present judgements, instead of being only a small or negligible part of the evidence that would be used by someone in such a situation, as the argument would demand, are in fact a major and important part of the evidence, if this evidence is described in accord with the phenomenalist policy. A supporter of the phenomenalist policy is, therefore, the one person who cannot use the argument reported above which was designed to show that present judgements could be removed from the scope of the general principle of the possibility of error.

The phenomenalist policy, that is, consists of taking memory judgements and analysing them into two parts, a judgement made now as to what was judged in the past and this latter judgement (which will be a present judgement). Errors may be allowed in memory judgement, but an error may be explained only by an error in the first of the two parts of the analysed judgement. Similarly, prediction is also analysed into two parts and an error may only be explained by an error in the first part, in the judgement about what the relevant present judgement is going to be. Present judgements, therefore, form a central part of all of someone's judgements about the world when these judgements are analysed according to the phenomenalist policy. Furthermore, they do not only enter into every judgement about how the world was, is, or will be but are also the part of every judgement that relates that judgement to the world. It is therefore quite impossible to exempt present judgements from the scope of the principle of the possibility of error when they are analysed in this way. If present judgements are analysed in accord with the phenomenalist policy, then it is quite easy to derive the intermediate feature that it must be possible for there to be error in present judgements from the features that have already been derived; and such a derivation means that a phenomenalist cannot carry out his whole policy, since it means that it must be possible for errors to arise exactly in the place where the phenomenalist is concerned to say that it is impossible for them to arise.

The basis of this argument designed to support the derivation of the intermediate feature, if that feature is understood in a phenomenalist way, can be used to support a more general argument in favour of the intermediate feature. It will be remembered that the principle of the possibility or error, proved in §18, is taken to apply in all areas of major importance, so that any area of judgement for which exemption from the scope of the principle is desired must be shown to be secondary in nature. It was shown above that this was just how present judgements could not be regarded if they were construed in accord with the phenomenalist policy. It must now be shown that this is how they cannot be regarded, however present judgements are construed. Then the intermediate feature will have been shown to follow from the other features that have already been derived.

Present judgements are an area of major importance on the phenomenalist policy because the phenomenalist policy arose from certain interests in perception. Since all judgements about the world were taken to be related to perceptual judgements, perceptual, and so present, judgements appeared as a component of all other judgements. If this perceptual preoccupation is ignored, however, there are much more natural ways to analyse the judgements that are not present judgements. For present judgements, it will be remembered, were originally taken to be those judgements in which the time at which the state of affairs judged was supposed to exist was the same as the time at which the judgement was being made. More obvious analyses of the other judgements to present judgements are, therefore, judgements which are made either before or after the time at which the state of affairs judged is supposed to exist. No memory or prediction of past or future perception is implied by such an analysis; the other judgements to present judgements are regarded, on the contrary, as just as straightforward judgements about how the world was or will be as present judgements are about how the world is.

The question now arises, therefore, of whether present judgements are still on this new, more natural, analysis an area of major importance in the protagonist's comprehension of his world. For it now looks as if the argument described above which was designed to show that present judgements could form a small minority of all judgements, or even that there might be judgement of a world without any present judgements at all might work in a way that it could not work when present judgements were analysed in accord with the phenomenalist policy. It seems, that is, perfectly possible that someone should just judge the past states of his world, describing everything after it had happened. It was objected above that on the phenomenalist policy this kind of case would not show that present judgements had a minor place, since all the memory judgements which such a person would use would contain present judgements. However, it looks as if, on the new analysis, this kind of case would show that present judgements might play an unimportant part in someone's judgement of his world since, on the new analysis, all the memory judgements that he relied on need not be thought of as containing a present judgement as part of themselves.

Such an argument, however, would be as ineffective on the new analysis as it was on the old analysis. To begin with, it ignores the fact that general judgements about the world, judgements about what laws hold in it, would have to be used or presupposed in making such retrospective judgements. These general judgements about the nature of the world would count on the new analysis as present judgements, being judgements about states of affairs supposed to obtain at the same time as that at which the judgements were made. More importantly, it would take more than mentioning such an example to show that present judgements have a secondary place to other judgements in a way which would exempt present judgements from the operation of the principle of the possibility of error. If they are to be exempted they must be shown to be essentially of secondary importance dependent on other major areas of judgement. Yet this example does not show anything like this, it only shows at best that they can be dispensed with in some cases.

No argument, in fact, can show that present judgements have, or could have, such an essentially secondary role. For on the new analysis, all judgements about the world have the same form, and in all cases they are direct assertions about what is in the world. The only difference is in the relation between the time at which the judgement is made and the time at which the state of affairs judged is assumed to exist. So, on the new analysis, present judgements are of the same status, position or importance as other judgements about the world. They therefore belong to the same major area of thought as the others do, and together they form the basis of anyone's thought about, and comprehension of, the world with which he is surrounded. So, on the new analysis, present judgements are not secondary to, or dependent upon, a more major part of someone's judgements, for on this alternative analysis all judgements have the same status, and yet, taken together, they form all the judgements there are about the world. No one kind of them, therefore, can be considered as secondary, and neither can they all be considered secondary to some other quite different kind of judgement. It is therefore impossible to represent present judgements as secondary on this new analysis of present judgements.

So on neither the phenomenalist nor on the new analysis of present judgements can present judgements be shown to be essentially secondary to other, more major, areas of a person's judgements of his world. Yet they would have to be shown to be secondary in this way if they were to be exempted from the scope of the principle of the possibility of error demonstrated in §18. This principle must therefore also operate for present judgements. This means that it must be possible for the protagonist of any comprehensible world to be in error in some of his present judgements; that is in some of the judgements he makes at the same time as the state of affairs judged is supposed to exist. Such was the intermediate feature that it was the concern of this section to demonstrate, and so it has now been shown that this intermediate feature follows from the other features that have already been derived.

§31   CONSEQUENCES OF THE POSSIBILITY OF ERROR IN PRESENT JUDGEMENTS

The general question which this part of the inquiry explores is whether there could be a comprehensible world composed wholly of sensations. It is whether, that is, a particular model world could be created which contained all the structural features discovered to be essential in any comprehensible world and yet in which all the objects of the protagonist of that world's judgements were sensations of the protagonist. This would be shown to be impossible if a feature could be derived from the features already shown to be essential which could not be contained in any world composed solely of sensations.   Such a feature is that the objects of a world must be able to exist unperceived. It was felt in §29, however, that it would be difficult to derive this feature from those derived already, and so it was decided instead to attempt to derive the feature that the protagonist could be mistaken in some of his present judgements since this seemed to be a hopeful intermediate step. This intermediate feature was accordingly argued for in the last section and shown to follow from features that have already been derived. In this and the next section, therefore, it must be seen whether any feature which could not be part of a world composed solely of sensations can be derived from the intermediate feature.

It will be remembered that the basic objects of traditional phenomenalist accounts had the twin properties of not admitting of error in present judgements about them and of not existing unperceived. These properties were probably felt to go together by traditional phenomenalists. If they are then the demonstration of the intermediate feature, which shows that such objects cannot be the only objects judged in a comprehensible world, might also be taken to be a demonstration that objects which cannot exist unperceived cannot be the only objects judged in a comprehensible world. For if the two properties are felt to apply to the same objects, then the demonstration that there must be objects which do not possess the first property could easily be taken to be a demonstration that there must be objects which do not possess the second property. This is another reason why a phenomenalist might be expected to resist the derivation of the intermediate feature that was examined in the last section.

It does not follow, however, from the fact that these two properties are felt to go together on some phenomenalist accounts that they are really related to each other in a way which means that an object which does not possess one of them cannot possess the other. It has been shown that it must be possible for the protagonist to be in error in some of his present judgements about his world. If, then, a world just of sensations is to be comprehensible, it must be possible for someone in such a world to be in error in some of his present judgements about sensations. However, this is not obviously impossible for, so far as the argument has gone to this point, it is not obvious that the possibility of error in present judgements means the possibility of the objects of those judgements existing unperceived. It may be natural to assume that the two properties go together, but it is not obviously essential.

It is natural to assume that the two properties go together since this is what seems to be the case in our own present world. Sensations like pains or tickles are felt not to have the second of the two properties in question since they cannot exist unperceived. So if I have a headache in the morning and again in the evening, I do not regard this as (numerically) the same headache which has reappeared again and which existed all day long, only unfelt by me. This is uncontroversial. What is interesting, however, is that sensations are held not to possess the first property in question either, since it is felt that present judgements about sensations cannot be mistaken. So if I say that I have a headache now, this is held to be the kind of statement I cannot be mistaken about. If I understand the language and am being honest, it is usually said, then what I say about my present sensations must be true. So for straightforward examples of sensations in our present world, neither of the two properties in question is held to be applicable.

On the other hand, it seems that both of the two properties in question seem to be applicable to objects of our present world like tables and chairs. So it is held to be possible that chairs can exist unperceived, but it is also held to be possible that I may be in error in my present judgements about chairs. I can judge, for example, that there is a chair somewhere where there is in fact no chair at all, or I can make mistakes in judgements about which properties a particular chair possesses.

In our present world, therefore, it seems that the two properties go together since it seems that either they both apply to an object, as happens for tables and chairs, or else that neither apply to an object, as happens for sensations. It is not surprising, therefore, that the demonstration of §30, that the intermediate feature is essential in any comprehensible world, should be taken as a demonstration of the impossibility of a world consisting just of sensations. For it seems to follow from the situation in our present world that there are two kinds of objects, those like sensations about which no mistake can be made and which do not exist unperceived and those like tables and chairs about which mistake can be made and which can exist unperceived. The demonstration of §30, therefore, that there must be objects about which mistakes can be made, may easily be felt to be a demonstration that there must be in any comprehensible world objects not only of the first but also of the second kind, that there must be objects, that is, which can exist unperceived.

This informal argument for a close connection between the

two relevant properties can be countered by an equally informal argument also using cases from our present world. This informal argument will be given in this section and then a more formal argument for the absence of connection between these two properties will be given later. The kind of case in our present world that looks as if it could cause difficulty for the idea that objects either possess both of the relevant properties or neither of them is a case where someone makes mistakes in judgements about something when he is looking at it in the best possible conditions of perception. For example, someone might look at a pen on a table clearly in front of him in the best possible light conditions and say, 'There is a pencil on the table.' Here he is obviously making an error in one of his present judgements, yet it is not clear that the object of the judgement exists unperceived. Of course, the object of the judgement is the kind of thing which can exist unperceived. However, it does not seem that it is unperceived on this occasion. Yet if such a case is possible, it means that the two properties of error in present judgement and of existence unperceived do not go so closely together as was supposed. For this case seems to be one of error in present judgement and yet not one of existence unperceived. It seems, therefore, that it may be possible to satisfy the requirements of the feature proved in the last section, the feature that it must be possible for there to be mistakes in present judgement, without introducing the feature that it must be possible for objects to exist unperceived. For it seems possible that every case of mistake in present judgement might be similar to the case just described, and so be a case of mistake in present judgement without being a case of existence unperceived.

It may be felt that this case of the pen judged to be a pencil really is a case of something existing unperceived. For it may be felt that the difficulty that this case seems to present only arises because of the difference between the two kinds of error in present judgements. It is only when things which do exist are judged not to exist that it is completely natural to say that something exists unperceived. It is not so natural to say this when something is judged not to possess a property which it does possess (for example, the property of being a pen). However, it is still possible to say in such cases that there is something about the world which is not perceived.

This is the natural thing to say in other cases of mistake about properties, for example in a case where a man says that a pen cunningly disguised as a pencil is a pencil. Here it is natural to say that something about the world, or more specifically about the pen, has not been perceived. For it has not been perceived that the object really is a pen. This case seems to be similar to the original one; and it seems quite correct to say also of the original case that it is a case in which something about the world has not been perceived. So in the original case, even if it could not naturally be called a case in which something existed unperceived, it could naturally be called a case in which something about the world was not perceived.

An attempt might be made, therefore, to argue for the desired feature of the possibility of existence unperceived by saying that it applies to the existence of properties, or of states of affairs of the world as a whole, as much as to the existence of individual objects. It would then be claimed that there would always be the former kind of existence unperceived in every case of error in present judgements, even if there is not always the latter kind of existence unperceived. So the argument would show that the possibility of some kind of existence unperceived follows directly from the possibility of error in present judgements.

This attempted argument seems justified in its assumption that not too much should be made out of the difference between the existence or non-existence of objects and the existence or non-existence of properties. For in many cases it is obviously arbitrary whether a judgement is taken to be asserting the existence of an object or asserting the existence of a property. Take, for example, the judgement 'Here is a peacock with a plume.' Here it seems to be arbitrary whether this judgement is taken to be asserting the existence of two objects (a peacock and a plume) or the existence of one object (a peacock) which has a certain property. So the attempted argument seems to be justified in its assumption that demonstrating the existence unperceived of properties is as good as demonstrating the existence unperceived of objects. Where the argument is less convincing is in its handling of the original case which was taken to demonstrate that mistake in present judgement did not imply existence unperceived, the case of the man in the best possible conditions of perception judging a pen to be a pencil. For in this case it seems very strange to say that something is not perceived, whether that thing be thought of as a separate object, as a property, or as a state of the world as a whole. The conditions of perception are perfect, and the person sees everything that is to be seen. It is just that he makes a mistake about it, once he has seen it. There is not something about the world that is not perceived by him. It is just that, having seen everything that is to be seen, the person makes a mistake in his judgement about it.

If it were claimed that in this case there was something about the world which was not perceived, it would be natural to ask what this thing was. The only possible reply would be that what was not perceived was that the thing on the table was a pen. This use of 'perceive', the 'perceive that' use, is a use in which perception is taken to contain certain elements of judgement; if someone perceives that something, they not only see it but judge it to be so. If someone sees something but does not judge it to be so, therefore, it will not be possible to say that that person sees that that thing is there. The reason for this, however, will arise from mistake in judgement rather than mistake in perception. In the case under discussion, therefore, in which it can be said that there is something about the world that the person does not see, this failure is caused by a failure in judgement rather than by a failure in perception. Yet this case is known to be a case of failure in judgement; what it was meant to show was that such failures in judgement involved some kind of failure in perception.

Informal examination of this case in which someone sees a pen in the best possible conditions of perception and judges that it is a pencil seems to show, therefore, that mistake in present direct judgement does not involve the existence of something unperceived. It might be felt that this was an unlikely case and that when it seemed to arise, we might always claim that the person had failed to perceive some property of the object in question. Take, however, another case. Two visitors to a wild-life park are engaged in intent study of the animals. One of them, after lengthy perusal of a rhinoceros, turns to his companion and says, 'What a magnificent hippopotamus!' Here he clearly makes a mistake in one of his present direct judgements about the world. Yet there seems to

be nothing in the world, or nothing about the world, that is
not perceived. There is clearly no object that he does not
see, a hidden hippopotamus for example. The rhinoceros is
quite openly there and he sees it perfectly clearly. Nor can
it be said that there is some property of the animal that the
person does not observe, such as its colour or how many horns
it has. All this the person sees perfectly clearly. Yet he has
made a mistake in present direct judgement about it. This,
therefore, is another case which shows that mistake in present
judgement does not involve the existence of objects unperceived. Looking at examples and arguing somewhat informally, therefore, it seems to be the case that the possibility of
mistake in present judgements, which was demonstrated in
the last section, does not imply the possibility of objects existing unperceived, which would show that no world just of
sensations could be a comprehensible one.

§32   LINGUISTIC AND OTHER ERRORS

The case of the pen and pencil and the case of the rhinoceros
and hippopotamus might be granted, and yet it might be
felt that they do not interfere with an argument from the
possibility of error in present judgements to the impossibility
of a world just of sensations. For it might be claimed that
the kind of error involved in these cases was merely linguistic
or verbal, and that this kind of error was a special case which
could be excluded from the main argument. It might be said,
that is, that the person in the first case just got 'pen' and
'pencil' confused and that the person in the second case just
got 'hippopotamus' and 'rhinoceros' confused. It might then
be claimed that it was assumed at the start that the person
understood the language, and so the possibility of cases arising
which were based on ignorance of the language were excluded. The claim, that is, is that two types of error can
be distinguished, real errors and merely verbal errors. Merely
verbal errors can be excluded at the start by the assumption
that the person in question knows the language. This leaves
real errors, and it can then be claimed that real errors in
present judgement imply the possibility of existence unperceived. So, this argument runs, we need only add the assumption that the protagonist understands the language in order
to turn the demonstration of the possibility of error in present

judgements of §30 into a demonstration of the possibility of existence unperceived.

This objection to the cases discussed at the end of the last section, and the consequent suggestion for admendment of the general argument, will not work. The objection would only apply, and the suggestion work, if understanding a language were a single, simple thing which could be assumed at the start of an inquiry and then forgotten about. It would only apply, that is, if the question of whether someone understands a language, and so the question of whether they might make verbal errors, is something that could be decided in advance of any particular case, and so is something which could not be relevant in any particular case. Yet this is obviously not so: it is impossible to guarantee in advance that someone will not make the kind of errors involved in the pen and the hippopotamus examples. Understanding the language is something which has to be assumed in every single case of judgement; and it is always possible that it may not be exhibited in any particular case. This means that it is not possible to eliminate the possibility of so-called verbal error in advance; and that such error is always a possible explanation of any particular case of mistake in judgement.

It is not just phenomenalists who have believed that it is impossible for a person to be mistaken about his own sensations. This is a very widely held belief, and it is because of it that it is quite natural to feel that the possibility of error in present judgements involves the impossibility of a world just of sensations. It is also the belief which has been depended upon by all those who wish to take judgements about sensations as forming the foundations of knowledge, and claim that judgements about other matters can be found to be true or false in so far as they can be reduced to, or at least connected with, judgements about sensations. Yet it is obviously possible for someone to misdescribe his sensations. Someone who holds that it is impossible to be mistaken about sensation statements, and that they form the foundations of knowledge, is forced, therefore, to distinguish between two kinds of error, verbal and real. Real errors are held to be impossible in judgements about sensation, and so these judgements can form the foundations of knowledge. Verbal errors are possible, but they form an unimportant special case. This distinction will only work, however, if it is possible to isolate verbal errors and eliminate the possibility of their occurrence in any judgement which it is desired to treat as foundational. If they cannot be eliminated in advance, and if it is always possible for them to arise in any particular judgement, then no judgement can be depended upon as being foundational. Yet this is exactly what the situation is: verbal errors cannot be eliminated in advance.

It is not claimed that it is impossible to draw a distinction between verbal and real errors nor that it is impossible to hold that errors in sensation judgements are always merely verbal. The point is, rather, one about how such a distinction can be made. It is obviously perfectly possible to tag an error as 'verbal' once it is found to be in a sensation judgement and to tag it as 'real' if it is not. However, this means of making the distinction will not enable the distinction to be used for the purposes for which it was introduced. It will not enable certain judgements to be treated as foundational, nor enable the proved possibility of present error support the possibility of objects existing unperceived. For either of these, it must be possible to isolate the possibility of verbal error in advance of any particular judgement. Since this cannot be done, the distinction will not perform the function desired of it. It is possible to make the distinction by fiat, and it is possible to disallow that sensation judgements can contain real errors by the device of calling all errors 'merely verbal'. Neither of these procedures, however, enables one to argue from the possibility of present error to the impossibility of a world just of sensations.

Since the impossibility of eliminating verbal error in advance is an important result with important consequences, it is worth looking at again in slightly more detail. This can be done with respect to a particular sensation word, for example 'pain'. People are usually taken to be the final authorities with regard to whether they are in pain or not. If they are sincere, and if they understand the language, it is usually said, then if someone judges that he is in pain there is no possibility of him being mistaken. This is the standard position, and it is normally held also that it is possible to check whether someone understands the language in advance of a particular occasion of its use. It can be checked, for example, whether someone is using 'pain' correctly by seeing whether he uses it in painful situations, by seeing whether he is tense, fidgety, or sweating, by seeing whether he attempts to remove himself from the situations which produce what he calls 'pain' and so on. Once such checking has taken place, the person in question is held to be able to understand the language; and it is taken that this can be regarded as established before his use of the language on a subsequent occasion. This is the standard position, and although it remains possible that such a tested person might subsequently lie, it does not seem possible that he should make a genuine mistake in one of his subsequent judgements. In this standard position the possibility of verbal error is eliminated in advance.

This standard position does rest on a correct assumption, which is that understanding a language is a dispositional property of someone, and so can be checked on widely separated occasions by the use (each time) of several examples and can be assumed to apply in the interim. However, what this assumption ignores is that it is possible to tell a mistake in judgement arising from a mistake in language on a single occasion, and to do it for a person who is known, on the evidence of other occasions, to understand the language. This is the only way, for example, in which the following case can be described. Someone is being consumed by fire, he is screaming and attempting to get away and is shouting out, 'I am not in pain.' This judgement is obviously false, and yet the falsity cannot be explained by him not feeling the pain that he is in. The only way, therefore, it can be explained is by saying that he made a mistake in language (the occasion being too terrible for insincerity). The same man may have shown on numerous other occasions that he understands 'pain' (or 'I' or 'not') so it is more natural to describe the case by saying that he forgot what 'pain' (or 'I' or 'not') were on this single occasion rather than that he did not understand them. Whichever way it is described, however, it still means that the question of a mistake in language may be vitally important in explaining a single case of judgement. So the question of understanding a language is not something that can be assumed at the outset of an inquiry and then subsequently be forgotten.

This case of the person in severe pain shows that even in

a case which is quite clearly a case of judgement about sensations, error is possible; and that this error cannot be guarded against in advance by any number of tests about whether someone understands the language or not. It is always possible to call such errors 'verbal errors', and this may indeed be the best thing to do. This does not alter the fact that it is not possible to eliminate such errors in advance, and that the possibility of error in present judgements does not imply the impossibility of a world just of sensations. This case of pain is a clear case both of a sensation judgement and of an error in present judgements. It is possible, therefore, to make a mistake in a present judgement without it being the case that there is anything about the case that is not perceived; the possibility of the former does not imply the possibility of the latter.

§33 FORMAL ARGUMENT FOR SAME CONCLUSION

In §31 certain particular cases were examined to see whether the possibility of objects existing unperceived followed from the possibility of error in present judgements. In these cases, the cases of the pen and the hippopotamus, it was found to be the case that there was error in present judgements and yet that nothing existed unperceived. It seemed, therefore, as far as it is possible to show something by such relatively informal examination, that error in present judgements did not imply that something existed unperceived. In §32 the suggestion was examined that all these errors were of one kind, verbal errors, and that once a distinction was made between verbal and real errors, the impossibility of a world just of sensations could be derived from the possibility of error in present judgements. It was seen that this distinction could not do the job that was demanded of it, and so that the one possibility did not imply the other. The time has now come to support this conclusion by arguments of a more formal nature.

One reason why it is natural to think that the one possibility implies the other is that in our ordinary use of English we take 'perceive' as having some sort of achievement or truth claim built into it so that if someone perceives something it follows that it exists. Conversely, if it does not exist, then the person does not perceive it. Mistakes in visual perception, for example, are reported in the form 'I thought I saw' just as mistakes in claims of knowledge are reported in the form 'I thought I knew.' If perception did not have this truth claim built in in the way that knowledge does, and were just a psychological state like belief, then such mistakes would be reported in the form 'I saw (wrongly)' analogously with 'I believed (wrongly).' Yet 'I saw (wrongly)' is as obviously incorrect as 'I knew (wrongly).' So, in our normal use of 'perceive' it appears to have a truth claim built into it. From this the claim naturally follows that a mistake in judgement implies that the object of judgement is not perceived. Thus it seems that ordinary usage supports the idea that the possibility of mistake implies the possibility of existence unperceived.

This argument could be criticized for the weight it lays on ordinary language. To say that mistakes in judgement imply the absence of perception just because one says 'I thought I saw' rather than 'I saw wrongly' is not necessarily any better an argument than saying that foxes do not have tails because one says 'a fox's brush' rather than 'a fox's tail'. However, it is not necessary to apply this criticism because the argument is formally invalid. Even, that is, if we assume that perception of an object implies the existence of an object, so that mistake about an object implies that perception has not occurred, it does not follow that something exists unperceived. Suppose someone mistakenly judges 'a' on a particular occasion. Since this is a mistake, there is not an a (on that occasion). On the ordinary language view, therefore, the person does not perceive a. (Since the view is that perception of a implies the existence of a, by contraposition the non-existence of a implies that there is no perception of a.) This, however, does not mean that anything exists unperceived. Ex hypothesi, a does not exist and so cannot exist unperceived. Yet nothing else has been mentioned and so there is no reason to say that anything else exists unperceived. So even though this is a case of mistake, it is not a case where it follows that anything exists unperceived.

In the case where a mistaken judgement, say 'a', is made, that is, all that follows on the ordinary language view is that it is not the case that a is perceived. Yet this does not imply that a exists unperceived, since it is quite compatible with there being no a to be perceived. This latter must indeed be the case, since the mistake in judgement shows that there is not an *a*. A particular example of this is the case of the rhinoceros and hippopotamus in §31. The fact that the judgement, 'Here is a hippopotamus', was mistaken shows that the person did not perceive a hippopotamus. It does not follow from this, however, that something, say a hippopotamus, exists unperceived. All that follows is that either a hippopotamus exists unperceived or that there is not a hippopotamus to be perceived. Yet it must be the latter possibility since the person was taken to be mistaken in his judgement that there was a hippopotamus. So it does not follow from the fact that a mistake has been made that there is anything which exists unperceived.

This argument from ordinary language, therefore, lends no support to the suggestion that the possibility of existence unperceived follows from the possibility of mistake in present judgements. The best way to demonstrate formally and finally that the one possibility does not imply the other is to decide whether a particular model world could be created in which all the objects of the world were sensations (or at least had the property of not being able to exist unperceived) and yet which contained the feature that error in direct present judgements was possible. Such a world can be taken to have total states of itself which succeed each other in a regular manner. It can be presumed that the protagonist continually perceives his world and so perceives all these states. Since they are states, or properties, of the whole world there is no question of their existence between two occasions in which the world is in a certain state any more than there is any question of the red of the traffic light existing between two occasions on which it is red. So here is a particular model world in which the objects of the protagonist's judgements can not exist unperceived. The question is whether it could contain the feature that error in direct present judgements must be possible.

This particular model world can contain this feature for exactly the same reason as the general model world contains it. Since the states of the world follow each other in a regular manner, there will be laws of this model world which express this regularity. Its protagonist, therefore, can use its laws in order to distinguish between his true and his false judgements. There will be sufficient power in his judgements of other instances, and his knowledge of the laws, to determine what the correct judgement of a particular instance should be, whatever he judges on that instance. There is therefore sufficient power to determine that a particular judgement made on that instance is false, whatever is judged in that instance. It must, therefore, be possible for this particular protagonist to make false judgements, and an argument similar to the argument of §30 can be made to show that it must be possible for this particular protagonist to make false present direct judgements. The same reasons as were used in the derivation of this feature in the general model world can be applied to this particular case. Therefore this particular model world contains the feature that it must be possible for the protagonist to be in error in his present direct judgements.

So this particular model world does contain this feature, and this is perfectly compatible with all the objects of the world being perceived. It will be remembered that in §29 there was a discussion about whether it would be possible to replace one process, perceiving, with another process, direct judging. It was decided that this was not possible unless 'judgement' was understood in a somewhat extended sense. It can now be seen that, whatever the answer to this question, the possibility of error does not imply the possibility of existence unperceived. On the first alternative, in which perception is equivalent to direct judgement, this means that (since all the objects in the particular model world are perceived) all the objects of the model world must be directly judged. Yet this is perfectly compatible with the possibility of mistake being made in direct judgement; it is indeed a precondition for it, since unless something is judged there cannot be a mistake made about it. On the second alternative, in which perception cannot be replaced with direct judgement, these two processes are quite independent of one another. It is, therefore, possible to combine any conclusions about the one with any condition of the other. This particular model world, therefore, may contain the feature that error in present judgements is possible while it is the case that all the objects of judgements are perceived. For if perception, whatsoever it is, is a completely independent state, it is obviously possible for the world to be in a certain condition of perception while it is in any condition of judgement. That all the objects of this particular model world are perceived, therefore, is compatible with the possibility of error in present judgements on this second alternative interpretation of 'judgement'. On both alternatives therefore these two are compatible and so this particular model world demonstrates that the possibility of objects existing unperceived does not follow from the possibility of error in present judgement.

It might be wondered why so much energy has been expended in establishing the conclusion that the one possibility does not imply the other. The reason is that the possibility of mistake in present judgements is an important result, which undercuts the basis both of most phenomenalist accounts, and also of many other theories of knowledge which rely on a foundation of perceptual judgements. This, and the picture of judgement that lies behind it, will be looked at more closely in the next section. It is equally important, however, to show that this possibility of mistake in present judgements does not imply the possibility of existence unperceived. For both the phenomenalists and their opponents have taken these two properties to go together, so that a demonstration that one is essential has been taken to be a demonstration that the other is essential; or a demonstration that one is not essential has been taken to be a demonstration that the other is not essential. The phenomenalists, for example, thinking that we can have experience of a world just of sensations, took judgements about these sensations to be judgements in which mistake was impossible, and so used present judgements about sensations as an incorrigible foundation for knowledge. On the other hand, those who wished to show that there were no incorrigible foundations to knowledge often took themselves to be refuting phenomenalism; and, alternatively, those who wished to attack the idea of incorrigible foundations often thought that this could only be done by attacking phenomenalism. All these attempts rest upon the mistaken assumption that the two properties in question go together. This is why it is important to demonstrate that the one property does not imply the other; and that the question of the possibility of mistake in present judgement (or of incorrigible foundations) is a quite separate question from the question of the possibility of existence unperceived (or of the truth of phenomenalism).

It is important to show, therefore, that the two properties do not imply each other. This means, on the one hand, that traditional phenomenalism cannot do what it attempts to do. For the demonstration of §30 of the possibility of error in present judgements means that it relies upon a mistaken view of the foundations of knowledge. If there are foundations, they are not absolutely incorrigible. There must always be the possibility of error in present judgements. It is possible to satisfy this condition using any kind of judgements, for example while using direct judgements or using perceptual judgements. Such judgements may also be normally taken as true, and so form practical foundations on which other judgements (for example, indirect or non-perceptual judgements) are based. Such foundations, however, are only for practical purposes; it must always be the case that any member of the class of judgements taken to be foundational might be mistaken. This means that there cannot be any absolute, or logically incorrigible, foundations. Traditional phenomenalism is therefore mistaken in thinking that it can use direct, present, perceptual judgements to play this role.

On the other hand, these mistakes in traditional phenomenalism do not mean that phenomenalism is impossible. For the proved possibility of error in present judgements has been found not to imply the possibility of objects existing unperceived. So far as has yet been shown, therefore, it is possible to have a comprehensible world consisting just of sensations. So far as has yet been shown, therefore, phenomenalism or idealism is still perfectly tenable. On the alternative language view, it has not yet been shown that there could not be a language describing only sensations and yet which says everything we wish to say about the world. The point of producing such a language may have been removed, since such a language can now no longer be taken to be describing the absolute foundations of our knowledge. There is nothing that has yet been shown, however, which means that such an alternative language is impossible.

So it has been important to demonstrate both the possibility of error in present judgements and also that this feature does not imply the possibility of existence unperceived. These demonstrations mean that it is possible to attack phenomenalism in a way which does not imply that a world just of sensations is incomprehensible. It shows that these are quite separate questions and can be handled separately. It distinguishes between those objections to phenomenalism which object to the view of the foundations of knowledge that it embraces and those objections to phenomenalism which object to it starting with sensations. This is an important distinction, and its consequences will be explored in the next chapter.

§34   PHENOMENALISM AND KNOWLEDGE BY
        ACQUAINTANCE

It has now been shown that the possibility of error in present judgements demonstrated in §30 does not imply the possibility of existence unperceived, and so does not imply the impossibility of a comprehensible world consisting solely of sensations. It has also been shown, however, that the demonstration of the possibility of error in present judgements nevertheless has important consequences for traditional phenomenalism; for, as was noticed in §29, one basis of traditional phenomenalism is the assumption that it is not possible for someone to be in error in his immediate present judgements about a world. This assumption can be attacked from a somewhat different direction from that used in the last sections. This is because it depends upon a picture of judgements having necessary objects. In this picture no judgement can be made without that fact alone producing, or guaranteeing, the existence of its object. This is taken to apply not just for a small, semi-accidental area of judgements about the world (such as, for example, token-reflexive judgements) but with regard to all the most important judgements about the world.

This picture, in which judgements have necessary objects, obviously allows no room for the possibility of false judgements. Yet the possibility of false judgements in general, and the possibility of false present judgements in particular, have both been found to be part of the general model world. These conclusions, perhaps, may be supported by a direct feeling of strangeness about the picture itself. For it seems that the whole point of making judgements about the world is that they may or may not correspond to their objects; that they assert that their objects are there but that they do not actually produce their objects. It seems, that is, that judgements are not in the world but, rather, describe what is in the world. Yet in the picture, where judgements are necessarily connected to their objects, it is as if the judgements were further objects in the world, almost as if they were different aspects of their own objects.

This is to describe, loosely and metaphorically, a feeling of strangeness about the picture which underlies the phenomenalist assumption of the impossibility of error in present judgements. It may, perhaps, be made more precise by considering the relation between the laws of a world and what the instances of those laws are immediately and independently judged to be. It was remarked in §18 that the protagonist must be prepared to take the dictates of the laws in preference to his immediate judgements of the instances. Yet this might be thought strange, particularly while examining a particular model world in which this is meant to operate. It may well seem strange, that is, that the protagonist must be able to take the judgement he can deduce from the laws, say 'y', as being true in a case where he immediately judges 'x'. For it might be thought that it would be more natural for a protagonist to follow his immediate judgements of the instances and for him to revise his laws in terms of the instances in cases of conflict.

This, however, would be to confuse what the protagonist of such worlds must do with what we would do in such a situation if the situation were only part of our present and complex world.

In particular, it is to confuse the kind of relation which holds between laws and the immediate judgement of the instances in the general model world with the kind of relation which holds between laws and the instances of those laws in science. In science, it is true, the instance is taken to demonstrate the falsity of the law and so, in cases of conflict the instance is preferred. This, however, can only happen because both instances and laws are part of a comprehensible world and because there is therefore, in general, no doubt about what the instances are.

In the general model world, however, the case is completely different because it is the conditions for such independent knowledge of, and correct judgement about, the instances that is being examined. So it is not how the relation between instances and laws could plausibly be described in a world like ours that is being examined but, rather, what the relation between the judgement of the instances and the use of the laws must be if there is going to be any judgement of the instances at all. In the former case the emphasis is on the instances and how they are best systematized by the laws; this is because the instances are assumed to be known and correctly judged. In the latter case, by contrast, the emphasis is upon what is essential if there is going to be any judgement of, or knowledge about, those instances at all. There are, therefore, two quite distinct kinds of relation here, one of which operates in science, and in which instances are preferred to laws in conflict cases, and the other of which the present inquiry is concerned with, in which it is demonstrated as essential that the judgement arising from the law should be preferred to the immediate judgement of the instance.

These two quite distinct kinds of relation, however, are confused together in the phenomenalist's picture in which every judgement has a necessary object. For here the distinction between judgements of instances and the instances themselves is diminished so that it becomes a matter of indifference which is discussed. There is consequently a temptation to regard as important only the type of relation which applies to things in the world, that is which applies to the instances themselves. This is the kind of relation between instances and laws which applies in science, and in which the instance is preferred to the law in conflict cases. In conflict cases, therefore, it is felt that the immediate judgement of the instance should be preferred to judgement arising from the law in the same way as, in science, instance is preferred to law. For on the phenomenalist's picture, with necessary objects for each basic judgement, it seems to matter little which is discussed. Different kinds of relation are, therefore, confused, and there is scope left neither for discussion of judgements as such nor for consideration of what is essential if there is to be judgement at all.

Once, therefore, the present inquiry is carried on, and it is considered what is essential if there is to be judgement at all, this means the end of the phenomenalist's picture of the necessary objects of judgement. It also means that a different kind of relation between laws and the instances of these laws is found to be essential. This is that, if there is going to be judgement at all in a comprehensible world, then what the laws determine the instances to be must sometimes be preferred to what those instances are immediately judged to be. Such a result has the consequence of underlining the destruction of the phenomenalist's picture, since it means that it is possible for present judgements to be mistaken, and so means that it is possible to have basic judgements without necessary objects.

The picture that has been destroyed in this way might be called the knowledge-by-acquaintance picture. This picture depends on the idea that all that is needed for knowledge of, and correct judgement about, an object is acquaintance with it. Such acquaintance is supposed to guarantee the correctness of judgements about the objects of acquaintance. This picture, or idea, depends upon the assumption that the immediate and independent judgement of one single instance can be known to be correct. It is assumed, that is, that a judgement can be known to have an object, and that it can be known that the terms used to describe the object are the correct terms, completely independently of any other judgement the judger happens to make. This assumption has now been exposed as false by the present inquiry. Yet its collapse entails the collapse of the knowledge by acquaintance picture, and so the collapse of the underlying picture of most phenomenalists.

After it was determined in §30 that error in present judgements must be possible, it was argued in §§31–3 that this did not imply that the existence of objects unperceived must also be possible. It can now be seen that the idea that the one possibility implies the other only arises if this phenomenalist's picture is still assumed even after the possibility of error in present judgements has been demonstrated. For the idea that the one possibility implies the other also depends on the assumption that certain judgements of central importance, perceptual judgements, have necessary objects. In the original phenomenalist picture, that is, all judgements of central importance about the world were assumed to have necessary objects. This picture has been destroyed by the result about the possibility of error in present judgements. Yet the idea that this possibility implies the possibility of existence unperceived depends on combining this particular result with a version of the original picture in which all perceptual judgements have necessary objects. For once this illegitimate combination is made, the result that certain central judgements do not have necessary objects becomes the result that certain central judgements are not perceptual judgements (since all perceptual judgements have necessary objects).

The argument against the idea that the one possibility implies the other may therefore be re-expressed quite simply by means of this phenomenalist picture of the necessary objects of judgement. If this picture can be assumed, then the one possibility does indeed imply the other. However, demonstration of the first possibility, which occurred in §30, shows that the picture is untenable. So this demonstration, while it provides the premiss from which one could move via the picture to the possibility of existence unperceived also removes the picture which is the only means of doing so. Pointing out the nature of this picture, therefore, not only shows why it is natural to attempt to argue from the one possibility to the other but also shows why it is impossible to do so. It also shows what is wrong with the phenomenalist's view of the nature of basic judgement and shows why there cannot be an account of knowledge which founds all knowledge on certain absolutely basic statements or judgements which are necessarily true, or necessarily connected with their objects.

§35 ANOTHER FEATURE

The feature that it must be possible to be in error in direct present judgements has been studied at length because of its particular interest in the study of phenomenalism. Although it has not led to a demonstration of the impossibility of a comprehensible world consisting just of sensations, it has shown what is wrong with the picture that many traditional phenomenalists have had of the world, and so has undercut the point of much phenomenalist enterprise.

Once attention is shifted away from phenomenalism, it seems that there might be more direct ways of demonstrating the impossibility of a comprehensible world consisting just of sensations. It may be, that is, that another feature can be

found which can be argued for in the same way as the intermediate feature and yet which, unlike the intermediate
feature, could not be possessed by a world which consisted
solely of sensations. To do this it is necessary to examine the
way in which the intermediate feature was demonstrated in
order to see how general this kind of argument can be made.

The crux of the argument for the intermediate feature was
the application of the general principle of the possibility of
error to a particular case. Now the general principle of the
possibility of error, in its turn, rests on the feature that it
must be possible to accept what an instance is judged to be
on the basis of the law in preference to what it is immediately
judged to be. The reason why this feature is essential is that
without it it would not be possible to isolate certain judgements as false, and so would not be possible to satisfy the first
premiss. So it must be possible to prefer the judgement based
on the law to the immediate judgement of the instance.
Another way of putting this is that it must be possible to tell
what an instance is, irrespective of what is judged on that
particular occasion. To take a particular example, if the laws
and the other particular judgements together all imply that
the state of the world at a particular time is x, then it does not
matter how the world is immediately and directly judged to
be at that time. If this direct judgement is 'x', then it is true;
if something else, then it is false. In both cases, however, it
is possible to tell quite irrespective of the direct judgement
what the state of the world on that particular occasion is.
If judgement based on laws and other instances were not
powerful enough to enable this to happen, they would not be
powerful enough to enable the protagonist to isolate false
judgements. In any world which is to satisfy the first premiss,
therefore, there must be sufficient power in judgements based
on the laws and on other instances for it to be possible to know
what one particular instance is, quite irrespective of what is
directly judged about that instance.

From this feature of the general model world, the possibility of error in present judgements was derived in §30. At
first this seemed to have the consequence that judgement
could not be just of sensations, for it is not usually thought
that direct present judgements about sensations could be
wrong. However, it has been seen in the last two sections that

this first assumption is mistaken. It could be the case that the protagonist of a world which contained this feature perceived everything in his world, and what he accepted when he preferred judgement based on law to direct judgement of an instance was the correct description of that instance. It is possible, that is, that the instance in question is perceived all the time and that the judgements, but not the perceptions, of it are changed. If this is so, then the necessity of preferring judgements based on law to immediate judgement of the instances does not seem to have the consequence that it must be possible for the objects of judgements to exist unperceived.

The question now arises of whether an analogous argument can be created whose consequences can not be avoided in this way. The following seems to be hopeful. In exactly the same way as the previous argument, there must be sufficient power in the laws and the judgements of other instances to judge a particular instance irrespective of what that particular instance is directly judged to be. This means that it must be possible to tell what an instance is, to tell what state the world is in at a particular moment, even if there is no direct judgement made about that instance, or state. In exactly the same way, that is, as the laws and the judgements of the other instances have the power to say the world is in state x no matter what is directly judged about it, they have the power to say the world is in state x, even if nothing is directly judged about it.

This argument depends on the assumption that it is possible to have a gap in a string of direct judgements. It seems that this obviously is possible (it happens in our own world for example) and it is easy to tell that such a gap has occurred from the protagonist's point of view. It would be possible for the protagonist of a particular model world, that is, to detect such a gap in much the same way as the protagonists of the particular model worlds described in Chapter Three detected mistakes. It will merely be a different kind of breakdown between the laws and the direct judgements, and one that seems just as possible. Once the possibility of a gap is allowed, then the point of the features derived above about the power of the laws is that it must be possible for the protagonist to tell indirectly by means of laws and judgements of other instances what is the case in a particular instance, even if he cannot judge that instance directly.

It seems possible to show, therefore, that it must be possible for the objects of a comprehensible world to exist without their being directly judged to exist. It must be possible, that is, for the world to be in state x (and this can be told on the basis of other direct judgements and the laws) even when the protagonist makes no judgements about what state it is in. So it is a further feature of the general model world that it must be possible for objects to exist without being directly judged. The argument, as has been seen, is strictly analogous to the argument for the feature that it must be possible for there to be mistake in present judgements. Both features follow from the feature that it must be possible to judge how the world is on a particular occasion on the basis of the laws and other direct judgements, and quite independently of what, if anything, is judged directly about that occasion. From this it follows that it must be possible both for there to be objects about which false direct judgements are made and also objects about which no direct judgements are made.

It is a feature of the general model world at this level, therefore, that it must be possible for objects to exist unjudged. The question is whether this implies that it must be possible for objects to exist unperceived, and so demonstrates that it is impossible to have a comprehensible world just of sensations. The question of whether existence unjudged implies existence unperceived was discussed in §29, and it was thought that it did not unless a very extended sense of 'judgement' was used. An example used there was a headache which continued all the morning and yet which was only judged to exist at 9 a.m. and 11 a.m. In the interim it existed un-judged, but it did not exist unperceived. So in this normal and relatively precise sense of 'judgement', existence un-judged does not imply existence unperceived. It is for 'judgement' in this sense that it has just been demonstrated that it must be possible for objects to exist unjudged (it being only for this clear sense of 'judgement' that it is obvious that a protagonist might or might not judge on a single occasion, or for which it can be asserted confidently that there might be gaps in a string of direct judgements). So this demonstration does not show that it must be possible for objects to exist unperceived, any more than the demonstration of the possibility of error in present judgements did.

On the other hand, if 'judgement' is taken in a very extended sense so that perception can be replaced with direct judgement, and existence unjudged implies existence unperceived, it is not so obvious that there could be gaps in a series of judgements or that the protagonist might or might not judge something on a single occasion. If 'judgement' is taken in this way, it becomes too wide-ranging and imprecise a notion for there to be any confidence about this. So if the possibility of objects existing unperceived is to be demonstrated, it is necessary to use some notion or sense of 'judgement' which is as precise and easy to handle as the narrower sense and yet for which existence unjudged implies existence unperceived. It does not seem, however, that there could be such a sense.

The situation seems different if the feature that it must be possible for objects to exist which could not be judged directly is considered, instead of the feature that it must be possible for objects to exist which are not judged directly. The latter has been seen either not to imply existence unperceived or else to involve so vague a notion that it is uncertain how it could be established. In its narrower or precise sense, it has been seen that it is possible for a headache to exist without its being judged. However, it does not seem that a headache could exist which could not be judged. For it seems to be a characteristic property of sensations that they are always available for judgement if the person whose sensations they are should wish to judge them. It seems, therefore, that if the feature that it must be possible for objects to exist which could not be directly judged can be demonstrated, then it will be possible to argue from it to the desired conclusion in a way that it is not possible to argue from the features already demonstrated.

This feature is obviously less precise than 'judgement' in its narrower sense. For although it can be supposed to be clearly demarcated whether someone judges something in this sense or not, it is obviously less easy to demarcate whether he could judge something or not. However, the rough idea is that someone is said to be able to judge something which he could judge if he thought about it, or which he could reply to questions about if asked. It is supposed, that is, that whenever it is said that someone could judge something there is no block external to himself to prevent him doing so; it is merely accidental that he does not do so, and nothing needs to be changed before he can do so. Take the headache example again. At 10 a.m. I still have the headache. Perhaps I am not thinking about it, but it seems perfectly proper to say that I could judge myself to have the headache; that nothing external needs to change before I am able to do so. On the other hand, if there is something that I am unable to judge directly, then this seems sufficient to show that this thing, whatever it is, is not a sensation.

It seems, therefore, that some control can be given to when something can be judged and when it cannot. Any argument using this concept is bound to be somewhat tentative, but on the other hand only by use of this concept does it seem possible to move from arguments and conclusions about judgement to conclusions about perception. The whole aim of this chapter, it will be remembered, is to demonstrate some feature which will have the consequence that a world consisting solely of sensations is an incomprehensible one. Features that can be demonstrated refer to judgement and the possibility of judgement. The only one that seems to offer any hope is the feature that it must be possible for objects to exist which could not be directly judged. For if this can be shown it seems to imply that it must be possible for objects to exist unperceived. This consequence does not follow if it is just shown to be possible for mistakes to be made in direct judgement about objects. For such mistakes might just be mistakes in description, misclassifications of clearly perceived objects. Nor does it follow if it is shown to be possible for objects to exist when no direct judgements are made about those objects. For objects that were being clearly perceived might not be judged, perhaps because the perceiver's attention was elsewhere. It does, however, seem to follow if it is shown to be possible for objects to exist which could not be judged directly. For it does not seem that an object can be said to be perceived if it is the case that it cannot be judged directly by the person supposed to be perceiving it.

Once this last feature is isolated as important it can be demonstrated in exactly the same way that the others were. First it has to be shown to be possible that there could be occasions on which judgements could not be made. This seems to be perfectly possible. It might happen, for example, at a certain time that a protagonist could make three direct judgements, at another time one, and at another time none. Whether or not a protagonist can make a direct judgement, that is, is just a matter of what he can do at any one time. It is a question of fact about his ability at that time, and is logically independent of all other considerations. So at any time it might be the case that the protagonist could not make a direct judgement at that time. It is therefore possible that there could be occasions on which direct judgements could not be made. This completes the first part of the argument.

Once it has been shown that it is possible that there are occasions on which direct judgements could not be made, then the rest of the argument proceeds exactly as in the previous cases. There is sufficient power in the laws and the judgements of the other instances to determine how a single instance is, irrespective of how that instance is directly judged to be. This will be the case whether the instance is directly judged wrongly, whether it is not directly judged at all, or whether it could not be directly judged at all. Whatever happens at the time of judging the instance, that is, it must be possible to tell quite independently what that instance is. It must, therefore, be possible for an object of judgement to exist whatever happens when that object is directly judged. So, as was shown above, it must be possible for objects of judgement to exist even when direct judgements are incorrect. So, as was also shown above, it must be possible for objects of judgement to exist even when there is no direct judgement about them at all. So, as can now be shown in an analogous manner, it must be possible for objects of judgement to exist even when the protagonist could not make direct judgements about them.

It must be possible, therefore, for objects to exist which can not be directly judged to exist. Yet it was claimed above that an object which exists which can not be directly judged to exist is an object which is not perceived. It must be possible, therefore, for objects to exist which are not perceived. This means that it is impossible to have a comprehensible world consisting just of sensations. For it is not possible for sensations to exist unperceived. Yet it has just been shown that it must be possible for the objects of a world to exist unperceived. The objects of a world, therefore, cannot all be sensations; or, in other words, a comprehensible world consisting just of sensations is impossible.

The desired conclusion that a world just of sensations would not be a comprehensible one has therefore finally been reached. The argument has been complex, and the key concept of objects which can not be directly judged is a difficult one to handle with certainty. Both of these factors mean that this conclusion must be less certain than some of the other conclusions derived in the course of the inquiry. In view of this, a much simpler and more certain argument for the desired feature will be given in the last chapter. In the meantime this argument demonstrates that it seems possible to derive this feature at the present level of the general model world. It also demonstrates that any argument for the feature at this level of the general model world is liable to be tortuous and uncertain, and that the feature does not follow from such more easily proved and obvious features as the possibility of error in direct judgement or the possibility of objects existing which are not directly judged.

CHAPTER SIX

Private Languages

§36 INTRODUCTION

A COMMON conclusion in present philosophy is that private languages are impossible. This conclusion derives from Wittgenstein and is usually thought to imply that a language which it would be impossible for more than one person to speak is not itself possible. Wittgenstein, it is true, introduces the question in §243 of the *Investigations* as if the question were whether a language which described someone's immediate private sensations was possible:

> But could we also imagine a language in which a person could write down or give vocal expression to his inner experiences—his feelings, moods, and the rest—for his private use?—Well, can't we do so in our ordinary language?—But this is not what I mean. The individual words of this language are to refer to what can only be known to the person speaking; to his immediate private sensations. So another person cannot understand his language (*Invest.*, §243).

However, Wittgenstein does allow that it is possible to speak of other people's sensations. His concern is not to deny its possibility but, rather, to examine what the preconditions are for such a possibility. This can be seen, for example, in the conclusion to §281: 'It comes to this: only of a living human being and what resembles (behaves like) a living human being can one say: it has sensations . . .' There is also no suggestion in Wittgenstein that it is possible to feel or have another person's sensations. For Wittgenstein, therefore, sensations are private in that they are only possessed by one person, yet they may be described by anyone in the common interpersonal language.

Since these are common assumptions of Wittgenstein, the direction of his argument against private languages can hardly be simply as an argument against the possibility of a language describing sensations which only one person can possess. The important point is, rather, that the language whose possibility is being examined is such that no one but the speaker can understand it (as in the last sentence of §243, quoted above, 'So another person cannot understand his language'). Such a language may be thought to have sensations as its objects, but this is not enough. It must also be about those sensations in a way that makes it impossible for it to be understood by more than one person, or about the kind of sensations which could not be described in a public language. This is the kind of language which Wittgenstein, and others, argue to be impossible.

Although Wittgenstein thinks that a language can be used to describe someone's sensations, he thinks that this is possible only because there is an intimate, a logical, connection between sensations and behaviour. It is obvious that he regarded the conclusion of the private language argument as that there could not be a language describing sensations for which there was no such connection. Such sensations could not be described in a common language, and Wittgenstein's concern is to argue that they could not be described in a private language either.

It is possible, therefore, to examine Wittgenstein's argument by examining a world just of sensations in which there is no thought of its objects being common to several people, nor of its objects being logically connected to something else (such as behaviour) which can be observed by several people. Wittgenstein's argument is in terms of language, but no more turns for him on the question of whether a language is possible than whether a series of judgements evincing comprehension of, and correct judgement about, the objects mentioned in such a language is possible. So it may be taken that the question of whether a world just of sensations is comprehensible or not has the same answer as Wittgenstein's question of whether a private language is possible or not.

This question was examined at length in the last chapter, and it was eventually decided that a world just of sensations would not be comprehensible. This obviously supports the conclusion of Wittgenstein's argument. It will be remembered also that the first premiss of the present inquiry is similar to the principle that Wittgenstein uses in this section of the *Investigations*, the principle that unless it is possible to distinguish between what actually is right and what merely seems to be so, then there is no point in talking about judgements being right at all. So the present inquiry not only produces a conclusion similar to Wittgenstein's but also starts from a principle similar to that employed by Wittgenstein. This, however, does not mean that the present inquiry necessarily supports Wittgenstein's argument. For just because it starts in a similar place as the argument of the present inquiry and ends in a similar place does not mean that Wittgenstein's argument is sound. However, it does mean that an excellent standpoint has been created by the inquiry from which to criticize Wittgenstein's argument and to decide whether it is sound or not.

Wittgenstein is not the only person to base an argument that private languages are impossible on the necessity of being able to distinguish between what is the case and what merely seems to be the case. This is also done, for example, by Shoemaker. He mentions Wittgenstein and remarks:

It is essential to the very notion of memory, as knowledge of an objective past, that there be a distinction between remembering something and merely seeming to remember something. And for there to be such a distinction there must be such a thing as checking up on one's memory and finding that one does, or does not, remember what one seems to remember (*Self-Knowledge and Self-Identity*, p. 252).

So Shoemaker also uses the same premiss in an argument that purports to show that this is impossible unless the utterances of other people can also be taken to be making memory claims. This is another example of a private language argument based on the first premiss of the present inquiry, and so another one that the inquiry is well placed to criticize. Both Wittgenstein's and Shoemaker's arguments will also be criticized later on internal grounds.

§37   CRITICISM OF THE ARGUMENT

In the private language argument it is claimed that some feature can be derived from the principle embodied in the first premiss of the present inquiry which could not be contained in a world just of sensations and which could only be contained in a world in which it was possible for there to be more than one person. It has been shown that a feature can be derived which could not be contained in a world just of sensations. This feature, however, makes no reference to the possibility of other people, and further argument would be needed to show that it could only be contained in a world which contained, or could contain, more than one person. So the inquiry only supports the conclusion of the private language argument in so far as this conclusion is taken to be the claim that a certain kind of experience, an experience just of sensations, would be incomprehensible. It does not support this conclusion when it is put in terms of privacy and publicity, or at least further argument would be needed to show that it would support it put in this way. This will be looked at later.

Once attention is shifted from the argument's conclusion to the argument itself, as presented, for example, by Wittgenstein, then the discoveries of the last chapter reveal important mistakes in it. For the crux of Wittgenstein's argument is that it is impossible to make the distinction demanded by the principle embodied in the first premiss in a world consisting just of sensations. He does not think that it would be possible, that is, for someone having the kind of experience he envisages in which sensations were not connected with something publicly observable like behaviour to make any kind of distinction at all between what was correct and what merely seems to be correct. In terms of the present inquiry, this is to argue that the first premiss immediately rules out as impossible the kinds of particular model worlds which have been described, in which a protagonist judges the states of the world with which he is surrounded.

Once this assumption or conclusion is put in terms of the present inquiry it can be shown to be mistaken. For it has been shown at length that it is possible to satisfy many of the requirements of the first premiss in a world consisting solely of sensations. As was seen in Chapter Three, it is possible for the protagonist of a world to distinguish between his true and his false judgements, his correct and his merely apparently correct judgements, if the objects of those judgements are so connected together that judgements about some of these objects support others of these objects. This was achieved by the laws of the particular model worlds, in which their states

were taken to succeed each other in regular order. There is
nothing, however, in this which could not be achieved in a
world just of sensations, for there is nothing to stop sensations
following each other in a law-like manner so that judgements
about one can be used to support or discount judgements
about another. Someone whose sensations followed each other
in such a way could use the judgement of one sensation to
make the difference between the judgement of another sensation actually being correct and its merely seeming to be so.

This possibility is not realized by Wittgenstein. Taking
as his model of the kind of language that he wants to show
impossible the case of someone who writes what his sensations
are down in a diary, he thinks that it is immediately obvious
that such a language could not satisfy the first premiss. For
it seems at first sight obvious that where there is no connection
between sensations and behaviour there could be no difference between 'S', say, being the correct description of the
sensation and it merely seeming to be the correct description,
no distinction between getting 'S' right and getting it wrong.
To establish such a difference, however, it is not necessary to
link sensations to behaviour or to make them commonly observable. All that is needed is to take another case where sensations follow each other in a law-like manner so that sensation
S, for example, is always succeeded by sensation T and preceded by sensation R. In this case there will be a difference
between actually getting a certain description correct and
merely seeming to do so by seeing what other descriptions that
this particular description is associated with. So in the case
Wittgenstein imagines of someone writing down sensations
in a diary, he could distinguish between 'S' being correct and
its merely seeming to be so by seeing whether it was preceded
in the diary by 'R' and succeeded by 'T'.

It is not, therefore, the case that a world just of sensations
is ruled out immediately by the first premiss. Of course the
first premiss has been seen to have many other consequences
than the law-like connection of the objects of judgement, but
it has been seen that many of these can also be satisfied in a
world consisting solely of sensations. For example, it was seen
to be a consequence of the first premiss that the protagonist
must be able to prefer judgements derived from the laws and
other judgements to the direct judgement he might make of

an instance. This means that it must be possible for him to be
wrong in his immediate direct judgements. It was seen, however, in the last chapter that it was possible also to satisfy
this requirement in a world just of sensations, once several
erroneous traditional views about judgement of sensation had
been eliminated. The argument from the first premiss to the
impossibility of a world just of sensations is by no means as
simple or direct as Wittgenstein makes it. Most consequences
of the first premiss could be accommodated in a world just of
sensations, and it needs the long and relatively tentative argument of Chapter Five before a feature can be derived which
could not be possessed by a world just of sensations. So when
the conclusions of this inquiry are used in criticism of the
private language argument, it can be seen to be defective.
Something like one way of interpreting its conclusion can
indeed be derived from its premiss; but it is not derived in
the way that the argument attempts, nor is its derivation as
simple as the argument assumes.

§38   AN ARGUMENT FOR INTERPERSONAL OBJECTS

It was claimed in §36 that it would need further argument
to show that the conclusion that a world just of sensations
was incomprehensible had any bearing on whether it must be
possible to have more than one person in the world. If this
can be shown, it will mean that the whole conclusion to the
private language argument can be demonstrated, even if the
argument is itself defective. An argument that might be
attempted is the following. It could be claimed that no sense
could be given to the supposition that someone was wrong
at a certain time unless someone else was right at that time,
or at least unless it was possible for someone else to be right
at that time. The claim here is that since truth involves
a correspondence, or at least a particular relation between
judgement and its object, there is no point in asserting that
such a correspondence, or relation, does not hold unless it
is possible for someone to see the lack of correspondence or
relation. Since, therefore, it has been shown that it must
always be possible for the protagonist to be mistaken in his
present direct judgements, this argument would claim that it
follows from this that it must be possible for there to be someone who could observe the lack of correspondence between

judgement and object involved in such a mistake. So this argument would conclude that it must be possible to have more than one person in a comprehensible world, and so uphold the conclusion of the private language argument.

The feeling behind this argument is that it cannot be certain that the objects of mistaken judgements exist unless it is possible for someone other than the maker of those mistaken judgements to perceive their objects and to make correct judgements about them. Consider, it might be urged, the case where the protagonist of a particular model world is confronted with the world in state x and mistakenly judges 'y'. Here the feeling is that the protagonist has no right to rely on his indirect judgement and to use the laws and his other judgements to deduce that the world is in state x unless it is possible for someone else to be confronted by x, and to judge directly that the world is in that state. If no one else could be in the world, and if the objects of the judgements could not be taken to be interpersonal objects, it might be urged, then the protagonist could have no right to be sure that he was in fact being confronted by x, and that his immediate present judgement was wrong.

This argument is obviously unsound. For it is obviously another argument which assumes the kind of phenomenalist picture which was discussed in §34. It is based, that is, on the idea that the objects of judgements may be directly known by acquaintance, that when they are so known no further guarantee for knowledge is required beyond the existence of the acquaintance situation itself, and that there is no other way of certainly knowing objects. The argument, that is, depends upon the idea that the protagonist can only be justified in his knowledge of the world when he is making true, present, perceptual judgements. He, therefore, can never be justified in knowing that the world is different from how he immediately judges it to be unless, at least, the objects of the world that he is in error about could form the immediate objects of someone else's knowledge by acquaintance. This is to accept the mistaken knowledge by acquaintance view which was discussed in §34, and the demolition of that view also demolishes this argument.

In fact, this argument is another case of trying to use the knowledge by acquaintance view in combination with another result which totally demolishes this view. For what the argument attempts to do is to combine this view with the conclusion demonstrated above about the possibility of error in present judgements. Yet it is just this conclusion about the possibility of error which totally demolishes the knowledge by acquaintance view. So the argument depends upon trying to run a pair of assumptions in harness, when one of these assumptions totally devours the other. The argument, accordingly, fails, and the desired conclusion cannot be attained. If the protagonist's use of his own direct judgements and the laws cannot enable him to judge a particular case, then there is no reason to suppose that the gap can be filled by anyone else's judgements.

In fact, the protagonist is justified in isolating certain of his judgements as false because he can bring to bear on them other judgements that he makes at other times by means of the laws of the particular model world that he is in. No other support is needed for certain judgements being false than this regular connection of the objects of judgement. Yet this regular connection of the objects of judgement does not depend on these objects being interpersonal, for it has been seen that such a connection can exist when the objects are sensations, and so are only available to one person. So there does not appear any way of arguing from the features that have already been derived to the consequence that it must be possible for the objects of a comprehensible world to be judged by more than one person. Yet this is what would be needed if the full conclusion of the private language argument (rather than one particular, and rather eccentric, way of interpreting it) were to be demonstrated by the present inquiry.

§39 WITTGENSTEIN'S ARGUMENTS

In §37 Wittgenstein was criticized for thinking that the impossibility of judgement just of sensations follows immediately from the first premiss of the present inquiry, and for not realizing that it would be perfectly possible to create some kind of distinction between a judgement's being correct and its merely seeming to be so, even if all judgements were just of sensations. It might be thought that this criticism is not fair in that it suggests that Wittgenstein's argument overlooks the possibility that sensations might be connected together so that judgements about certain sensations could be used as evidence for the truth or falsity of judgements about other sensations. For Wittgenstein does consider the possibility of using the connection together of memories to provide evidence for the truth or falsity of judgements in a private world. In §265 of the *Investigations*, for example, he lets his imaginary interlocutor make such a suggestion. The argument of that section in full is as follows:

Let us imagine a table (something like a dictionary) that exists only in our imagination. A dictionary can be used to justify the translation of a word X by a word Y. But are we also to call it a justification if such a table is to be looked up only in the imagination?—'Well, yes; then it is subjective justification.'—But justification consists in appealing to something independent.— 'But surely I can appeal from one memory to another. For example, I don't know if I have remembered the time of departure of a train right and to check it I call to mind how a page of the time-table looked. Isn't it the same here'—No; for this process has got to produce a memory which is actually *correct*. If the mental image of the time-table could not itself be *tested* for correctness, how could it confirm the correctness of the first memory? (As if someone were to buy several copies of the morning paper to assure himself that what it said was true.)

Looking up a table in the imagination is no more looking up a table than the image of the result of an imagined experiment is the result of an experiment.

Here the interlocutor makes the suggestion that justification can be provided by appealing from one memory to another. Wittgenstein replies that this will not be justification since justification cannot be provided by the same kind of judgements as the judgement that is to be justified; on the contrary, justification must appeal to something independent and produce a judgement that is actually correct. Wittgenstein's argument, that is, is that the other memories that are appealed to come from the same tainted source as the memory that is being tested. These other memories could only be used in justification, he argues, if they could themselves be independently justified. So while I might support one memory or judgement of sensation by another, this support is only possible because I can support the second by appealing to something independent, by appealing to judgements about a common world of interpersonal objects. Judgements of sensations or memories can only be supported by appealing to judgements about interpersonal objects, and if in a particular case one judgement about sensation or memory is supported by another, this is only because in that particular case this other judgement or memory is supported by such judgements about interpersonal objects.

The passage quoted at length above is sometimes translated (for example, by Hintikka in *Mind*, 1969) so that instead of claiming that justification has to produce a memory that is actually correct justification must be able to produce the *right* memory for it to be the case that one memory could support another. The relevant point, however, remains much the same. An interpersonal standard is needed if there is to be real justification, and this cannot be provided if appeal is from one memory to another. Only if judgements of interpersonal objects are used in justification can it be certain that the justification depends upon judgements that are correct, or certain that the right judgements are being used in the justification. The spirit of §265, particularly on Hintikka's interpretation, occurs also in §259: 'Are the rules of the private language *impressions* of rules?—The balance on which the impressions are weighed is not the *impression* of a balance.' This has the same implication. Although it might be possible for someone to associate together his impressions in order to sort out which of them were correct and which were not correct, he could only do this if there were an external and objective standard by which they could be associated with each other. Again the supposition is that this can only be provided by judgements of interpersonal objects, by judgements of an external, objective world. Only if such judgements were possible, could there be judgements known to be correct on which justification might be based, could it be known that the right judgements were being used in justification, and could it be known how judgements should be associated together so that some could be isolated as true and others as false.

These are the further steps in Wittgenstein's particular argument which were ignored in §37. To the claim embodied in the first premiss, which it was seen did not result in the impossibility of a world just of sensations in the way Wittgenstein suggests, he adds the claim that there is no real justification unless justification can rely on judgements that are known to be correct, or unless it is known that it is the right judgement that is being used in justification. Wittgenstein thinks that this only happens if at least some judgements are of interpersonal objects, and so considers a language consisting only of judgements of private objects to be impossible. Unfortunately for his argument, however, the arguments that he uses against the possibility of associating together memories or judgements of sensation in order to find which are right and which wrong are also arguments which will work against the possibility of our discovering which judgements are right and which wrong in our own interpersonal world. For in our present judgement of interpersonal objects it is impossible to select certain judgements as being automatically correct, or as being the right ones to use in justification. We justify judgements about such interpersonal objects in the same way as it was suggested that justification could be carried on in a world just of sensations, that is by associating together the judgements we make in accordance with the laws of our particular world. We cannot start with particular judgements which are certainly known to be correct. There is no appeal to something independent, or completely outside the system.

In both the present world and also the kinds of particular model world that were discussed in the last chapter the truth or falsity of individual judgements can be discovered by associating judgements together in accordance with the laws of that world. Yet in neither case can use be made of judgements automatically guaranteed to be correct, or of laws guaranteed to be correct (so that it could be known automatically that the laws were not impressions of laws, and so known automatically which was the right judgement to use on any particular occasion of justification). This means that both certain private worlds and also the present public world can satisfy the first premiss in that it is possible to make some distinction between true judgements and false ones, between a judgement being really correct and it merely seeming to be so. Now someone might wish to add to the requirement embodied in this premiss the additional requirement that it must be possible to be absolutely correct in judgement, that judgements and laws can be used which are known to be right. This Wittgenstein does in later stages of his argument, and it does have the desired result of eliminating private languages. However, this additional requirement would also eliminate our present public world as incomprehensible if it were adopted, which is absurd.

As far as Wittgenstein takes the first premiss, therefore, it is perfectly well satisfied by some private worlds as well as the present public one. These private worlds would not satisfy an additional requirement that Wittgenstein suggests. This additional requirement, however, cannot be a serious requirement of any comprehensible world since, if it were, it would result in our present public world being considered incomprehensible. It is true that it seems that certain consequences of the first premiss could not be satisfied in one particular kind of private world, a world consisting just of sensations. This, however, needs a long, complicated argument and is not something that is shown by Wittgenstein.

§40 SHOEMAKER'S ARGUMENTS

The criticism of the private language argument based on the conclusions of the present inquiry which was conducted in §37 can be reinforced by a more detailed examination of Shoemaker's arguments. Shoemaker, as was remarked in §36, starts with the premiss that someone must be able to distinguish between how things seem to him and how they really are. He argues from this to the following conclusion:

Unless I am willing in some circumstances to accept the utterances of other persons as memory claims, and as evidence concerning what has happened in the past (among other things, what has happened to *me* in the past), and were willing to do this without first having conducted an empirical investigation to determine whether I am even entitled to do it, I would in effect be admitting no distinction between the way things are and the way they seem to me to be . . . (*Self-Knowledge and Self-Id.*, p. 254).

This obviously forms a private language argument, starting again from the first premiss of the present inquiry.

Shoemaker also considers, while conducting the argument, the possibility that I could distinguish between how things were and how they merely seemed to me to be by associating my memories together: 'Perhaps it will be said that I can know that one of my memories is mistaken by seeing that it conflicts with the rest of my memories' (p. 253). He replies to this that I could not know that they conflicted on the basis of my experience alone, for there can only be such conflicts in judgements or memories when they are about such things as tall buildings (his example). So far this argument takes the course that Wittgenstein's followed in the last section; I might be able to correct some of my memories or impressions by others but that is only because there is an objective balance in judgement of the interpersonal world with which such memories or impressions can be weighed.

Shoemaker, however, imagines further objections and difficulties for himself and it is his argument with respect to these that makes it worth considering him separately. It was objected in §37 that Wittgenstein's private language argument ignores the possibility that sensations could be connected together in a law-like way so that it would be possible to distinguish between a judgement about a particular sensation actually being correct and its merely seeming to be so. Shoemaker, unlike Wittgenstein, considers this possibility: 'But could *my own* past experience, or rather my present memory of it, be sufficient to give me the general knowledge of the world, of causal laws and so on, that I would need in order to be able to conclude from what I seem to remember that one of my memories is false?' (p. 253). Yet although Shoemaker considers this suggestion he does not regard it as a genuine possibility and replies to the question just quoted, 'I think not.' He thinks what it would be like if I did attempt to frame generalizations about the world based on my past experience and tried to use these generalizations to isolate certain judgements or memories as false. He objects that: 'there is no reason why I cannot make these generalizations complicated enough to be consistent with all my memories' (p. 253). If this is an argument, however, then it is another argument which would also exclude the present world if it were applied to it. For there is no reason in our present world in which we can use other people's memories why we could not make our laws so complex that they would cover all the judgements made about the world and memories of everyone. With such laws it would be impossible to isolate anybody's judgements or memories as false or to distinguish for anybody between what was actually the case and what merely seemed to be the case.

This argument of Shoemaker should in fact be stood on its head. For, since nobody in our present world could distinguish between what seems to be the case and what actually is the case if this possibility of the law covering all the memories is allowed, this means that (if this distinction is to be made) this possibility cannot be allowed. It is not enough that there should be laws; it is also necessary that these laws be sufficiently simple to isolate some judgements that have been, or could be, made as false.

Shoemaker shows some awareness of this (although he may think himself to be making a further objection) for he goes on: 'To be sure, if I try to make my generalizations fairly simple, I shall probably find it impossible to make them consistent with all my memories' (p. 253). Even with simple generalizations, however, Shoemaker thinks that the memories of other people are essential if I am going to be able to distinguish between the memory judgements that I make which merely seem to be correct and the memory judgements that I make which actually are correct. For Shoemaker thinks that there is a flaw in the policy of adopting the simplest, or of adopting simple, generalizations:

But suppose that I have formulated a set of relatively simple generalizations that are consistent with a majority of my memories, but inconsistent with a small minority of them. Can I conclude that the recalcitrant memories are false? Is it not possible that I could formulate a different set of generalizations, equally simple, that would 'save' an equally large but different set of my memories, so that memories that would be 'false' according to the first set of generalizations would be 'true' according to the second set, and vice versa? (p. 253).

Here again, however, if this argument works against the possibility of one person using simple laws to distinguish between his merely apparent and his true memories, then it also works against the possibility of all of us using laws in order to distinguish between our merely apparent and our true memories in our present world. For, assuming that we do use generalizations about the world in order to distinguish between our true and our false memory claims (and Shoemaker accepts this, giving as an example a case of deciding between memories by using 'a general truth I know about the world, namely that tall buildings cannot be built in a day' (p. 253)), then this procedure would also be impossible in our present world if there could be two equally simple sets of generalizations, each of which isolates different judgements as 'false'.

If, that is, the possibility of two equally simple sets is a conclusive objection to the device of using simple, or the simplest, set of laws, then it is a conclusive objection to our present practice in the public world. Therefore, if the argument is valid, it not only eliminates the candidate Shoemaker wishes to eliminate (using the connection between one person's memories, as expressed in laws) but also the candidate Shoemaker wants to replace it with (using the connection between everybody's memories, as expressed in laws). Such an argument cannot be valid, or at least could not properly be thought by Shoemaker to be valid. It cannot, therefore, be used to show that a person could not distinguish between his true and his false memories by use of his own memories alone.

Here, again, Shoemaker's argument should be stood on its head. He proposes a particular difficulty about using simple laws, which he thinks applies only in the case of one person judging his own memories unaided by the memories of others. However, since this difficulty would also occur in the public, interpersonal case, it can be seen that what Shoemaker has found is a general requirement which must hold in any world in which laws are to be used to distinguish between true and false judgements. This is that there must not be two equally simple accounts covering the whole of experience, yet different from each other. Shoemaker, therefore, has pointed to a further requirement that any world must satisfy if it is going to be possible to distinguish between true and false judgements in it. Yet this is not a requirement which could not be satisfied in a wholly private world, which could not be satisfied, for example, in the particular model worlds which were described in the last chapter. Pointing such a requirement out, therefore, does not form part of a valid argument against the possibility of someone distinguishing between his true and his false memory claims by means of simple laws

asserting connections between the objects of those judgements, even if such objects are completely private to him.

Shoemaker next comments: 'Just as the concept of a true
account of reality, of how things are and have been, is different from the concept of how things seem *to me* to be and to
have been, so also is it different from the concept of the
simplest account consistent with most of *my* experiences, or
with most of *my* memories' (pp. 253–4). This marks a change
of direction in the argument. For the aim of the argument is
to show that it is impossible that there should be any distinction between how things are and how they seem to me to be
if I only consider my memories. The aim, that is, is to show
that someone could not isolate his true memories unless he
could use the memories of other people, or at least use objects
and laws that could appear in the memories of other people.
Yet this present comment makes quite a different kind of
objection, which is that someone who only uses his own
memories will not be as successful as someone who also uses
the memories of other people, and will sometimes fail to make
a distinction between true and false memories which should
be made. This is quite a different matter and irrelevant to
the main argument and its intended conclusion. It is quite
true that someone in an interpersonal world who uses only
his own memories will do worse in his judgements of that
world than someone who uses everyone's memories. This,
however, is not because there is something necessarily
deficient about using one person's memories, but simply
because he is not using all the evidence that is available to
him in the world he happens to be placed. It does not form
an argument to show that it is impossible for one person using
just his own memories to distinguish between true and false
memory judgements.

Detailed examination of Shoemaker's arguments, therefore,
shows that he has not demonstrated the necessity of there
being more than one person in a comprehensible world, or
the necessity of the objects of at least some judgements being
interpersonal. He makes several objections to a private use
of justification and a private ability to make the distinction
between judgements merely seeming to be correct and their
actually being so. However, in the way these objections are
made, they are also objections to our present public use of

justification or our present drawing of this distinction. What Shoemaker has really discovered are several conditions which must be met by any world in which justification, or this distinction, is to be possible. Yet there is nothing to prevent a wholly private world meeting these conditions; pointing these conditions out does not show wholly private worlds to be impossible.

§41 PUBLICITY AND PRIVACY

Examination both of the particular arguments put forward by Wittgenstein and Shoemaker, and also a comparison of their conclusions with the conclusions reached in the present inquiry has shown the private language argument to be mistaken. It is true that the inquiry eventually reached the conclusion that a world just of sensations, which is an important case of a wholly private world, is impossible. The inquiry, however, reached this conclusion without any reference to publicity or privacy, nor is it clear how this conclusion can be made to produce any results about the possibility or impossibility of wholly private worlds. It is clear that the main point of the private language argument is to show that a world just of sensations could not be a comprehensible world. However, it now also seems clear that the wrong way in which to achieve such a result is by consideration of privacy or publicity as such; if a world composed wholly of sensations is impossible, it is not impossible because it is a wholly private world but because it would not be possible for objects to exist in it which could not be directly judged by its protagonist.

It was observed in §36 that both the inquiry and Wittgenstein's argument agree in the conclusion that a world just of sensations is impossible. It was then commented in §37 that part at least of the difference between the two arguments was that Wittgenstein thought that this conclusion followed immediately from the first premiss of the present inquiry, while in fact it takes a long and complex argument from the first premiss in order to arrive at this conclusion. If, however, the argument is not taken to be about the impossibility of a world just of sensations as such but, rather, about the impossibility of a world or experience consisting solely of sensations such as they are in the present world, then the two arguments are closer to each other. For it follows both from Wittgenstein's argument and also from some of the first and most definite conclusions of the present inquiry that there could not be comprehensible experience consisting just of sensations like sensations in our present world. In Wittgenstein's argument this is because such sensations are private. According to the first conclusions of the present inquiry, it is because sensations as they exist in this present world do not exhibit the kind of order and connectedness that there has to be between the objects of any comprehensible world. Such order and connectedness is taken over by interpersonal objects in the present world and these therefore become the essential basis in it for distinguishing between how things seem to be and how they really are. So according to both Wittgenstein's private language argument, and also the first and most certain conclusions of the present inquiry, a world consisting just of sensations similar to sensations in our present world lacks a necessary condition for it being a comprehensible world, a condition furthermore which is provided by the interpersonal objects of our present world.

This is interesting when the generally descriptive cast of Wittgenstein's philosophy is remembered. For although on the face of it Wittgenstein is arguing that private languages, or comprehensible experience just of sensations, are absolutely impossible, his concern may be rather to show that the kind of private language we could have in our present world, or comprehensible experience of the kind of sensations we have at present, is impossible. If it is, then his argument is less far from the inquiry than seemed at first sight. For it follows as a direct consequence of the first premiss in either case that such experience would not be possible; in Wittgenstein this is because it would not be of public objects, in the inquiry it is because it is of objects which (not necessarily, but as a matter of fact) are not sufficiently connected together.

It may, therefore, be possible to effect a certain *rapprochement* between Wittgenstein's argument and the argument of the inquiry. This, however, does not alter the fact that Wittgenstein's argument is a misleading and, at least on the face of it, incorrect way of making the central point. For Wittgenstein's argument is about privacy and publicity, and this draws attention to the wrong feature in a decision that an experience of our own present world is comprehensible and that an experience just of sensations such as we have at present would not be comprehensible. For the reason that such an experience would not be comprehensible is that the objects of judgements about such experience would not be connected together; and this is the condition that is met by public objects in our present world. This is the important feature, and the one that has been discovered in the present inquiry. To draw attention to privacy and publicity is irrelevant and potentially misleading. In the case provided by sensations such as they are in the present world the two ways of distinguishing between comprehensible worlds and incomprehensible ones overlap. However, they only overlap as a matter of fact; the world which lacks the essential feature of connectedness happens to be a private one also. It is not necessarily going to be the case that the two features will go together, and if they separate it is the feature of connectedness that will be looked at to decide whether a particular world is comprehensible or not. Bringing in privacy and publicity is just irrelevant.

It might be argued that when all the features necessary in a comprehensible world are discovered, it will also be discovered that such a world must be a public one, must be a world containing interpersonal objects. This may be the case, but it has not been shown yet. What has been shown is that there is not the direct sort of argument for the necessity of a public world that Wittgenstein and Shoemaker attempt to produce, and that therefore this is the wrong way to produce an argument showing that a world consisting just of sensations is impossible. When Wittgenstein attempts to produce such an argument he forgets that it is possible for a world just of sensations to fulfil the requirements he sees to be necessary. It is true, of course, that a world consisting of sensations exactly like sensations in our present world would not fit such requirements, but this is because of the overlap in this particular case of the feature Wittgenstein is interested in, privacy, with the feature that the inquiry has shown to be important, lack of law-like connectedness. This is a merely contingent association of the two features, and does not show that the association is necessary This just reinforces the point that the important features to look at are features such as law-like connectedness, the features in fact which have been derived in the present inquiry. Talk of publicity and privacy bears no essential connection with them that has yet been demonstrated, and seems to be just a red herring.

Although, therefore, as things are, Wittgenstein's results will be true at the same time as the results of the inquiry, this is purely accidental. Talk about privacy and publicity is misleading. What is essential and important is the feature of law-like connectedness, and the related feature of the possibility of error. It is the absence of these which show a world to be incomprehensible, and there seems to be no obvious connection between them and the features of privacy and publicity. In particular, it seems to be possible for a wholly private world to be connected together in a law-like manner. Wittgenstein, therefore, concentrates on the wrong feature in his investigation. His attack on the possibility of private languages does not succeed; and consideration of privacy is in any case the wrong way to attack traditional empiricism or phenomenalism.

CHAPTER SEVEN

Space and Action

§42 INTRODUCTION

In the last chapter the connection between the features of being potentially public and of being law-connected was discussed. It was noticed that in the particular case of the present world, the objects that were law-linked, and so satisfied one of the essential conditions of the world being a comprehensible one, were also the objects that were interpersonal. On the other hand, the objects that were private were not law-linked and so could not be the sole constituents of a comprehensible world. It was suggested that this was a reason why someone (for example, Wittgenstein) might think that these two features were more closely connected with each other than they really were; and it was argued that if attention was kept on the features themselves, rather than how they were connected in this one particular case of the present world, it would be seen that they were not necessarily connected, or at least that further argument would be needed to show that they were.

It is inevitable, however, that the way features are combined in the one particular world that we can easily observe, our own present world, should provide suggestions about how these features are essentially connected together. It is interesting to notice, therefore, that the objects which are law-connected in our present world, and so meet the first essential condition for a world being a comprehensible one, are not only the objects which are public but are the objects which can exist unperceived and the objects that are connected together with each other and with us in a spatial system. This must raise the question of whether it is not an essential feature of any comprehensible world that its basic objects, or at least some of its objects, should be able to exist unperceived and should be spatially connected with each other and with their perceivers. The first part of this question was given an answer in §35, when it was argued that it was an essential feature of any comprehensible world that its objects should be able to exist unperceived. The chief aim of this last chapter is to consider the second part of this question. It is to consider, that is, whether it is an essential feature of any comprehensible world that its objects should be spatially linked with each other and with their perceiver. This is a feature, along with publicity and the ability to exist unperceived, which is possessed by the basic objects of our own present world (by the objects which fulfil some of the most essential conditions of a world being a comprehensible one). It must now be seen, therefore, whether the conjunction of these features in this present case is merely accidental, or whether it reflects an essential connection between the features themselves.

It was shown in §21 that either space or time was essential in any comprehensible world. However, in Chapter Four, time was first argued for and then assumed with the introduction of an extra premiss. This means that if space is to be shown to be an essential feature of any comprehensible world, then this will have to be shown by independent argument and cannot just be taken to follow automatically from the demonstration of §21. In any case, either time or space was seen to be required in §21 because it was realized that there had to be a way of separating qualitatively similar instances, of saying when there were two instances of something rather than one. Even if this was not done by time, it might be the case that it could be done by a different kind of spatial connection from the one argued for in this chapter, which is that objects should be spatially connected with each other and also with their perceiver. For this would be accomplished if there were merely spatial connection between the objects (or some of the objects) themselves and there was no question of any spatial relation holding between the objects and their perceiver.

The point here is the following. Suppose that there is an after-image which consists of two exactly similar halves. These halves can be regarded as different objects of judgement, can, that is, be separated in judgement from each other. Yet, because they are exactly similar, this cannot be done by their purely qualitative properties (done by one being red and one being green, for example). Nor can it be done by differences in the temporal relation between the two halves and the objects of other judgements. For the two halves exist simultaneously, and can be supposed to appear and disappear together. The separation in judgement between them, therefore, must be based on another dimension apart from time, must be based on some kind of spatial relation existing between the two halves of the after-image. One half, that is, can be thought of as above the other, or as being on its left. Yet an after-image may be taken as a model of a sensation, so that there can be no question of it existing unperceived. It is possible, therefore, for spatial relations to exist between objects for which there is no question of them existing unperceived and which are not public. In such a case, however, although there is a spatial relation between the parts of an object, there is no spatial relation between those parts and the person perceiving (or experiencing) this object. The kind of spatial relation, therefore, which exists for the public objects of our present world which are law-linked and able to exist unperceived is a relation not merely between the objects themselves but also between the objects and the people who perceive them. This, therefore, is the kind of spatial relation which is to be argued for in the present chapter.

It is hoped to demonstrate that it is an essential condition of any world being a comprehensible one that its protagonist is spatially related to at least some of the objects of his judgements. The interest in this feature is that it is possessed by the basic objects of our present world. It is also a feature which is likely to connect very closely with the possibility of objects existing unperceived. For it need only be presumed that the protagonist can only perceive the objects that are close to him in space, or at least that perception of the objects that are close to him in space interferes with and in some cases prevents perception of the objects that are further away, for it to be the case that the possibility of existence unperceived follows directly from the protagonist being at a particular spatial position in his world. If, therefore, the feature that there must be spatial relations between the protagonist and the objects of his world can be demonstrated, it should be possible to provide a simpler and more certain argument for the possibility of objects existing unperceived.

§43   EXISTENCE UNPERCEIVED AND SPACE

If the possibility of objects existing unperceived follows from the feature that the protagonist is at a certain spatial position in his world, this does not mean that the feature that the protagonist is at a certain spatial position follows from the possibility of existence unperceived. The implication, that is, may hold in the one direction but not in the other. If this is so, the possibility of existence unperceived could be a feature of the general model world without it also being a feature of the general model world that the protagonist should be in spatial relation with the objects of his world. This, in fact, is what seems to be the case, and so blocks a direct argument from the conclusion of §35 that it must be possible for the objects of a comprehensible world to exist unperceived to the desired conclusion of the present chapter that the protagonist of a comprehensible world must be in spatial relation with the objects of some of his judgements.

The argument for the conclusion that it must be possible for the objects of a comprehensible world to exist unperceived depended on noticing that the power of the laws and the direct judgement of other instances had to be such that they provided a sufficient basis for the indirect and true judgement of any one particular instance, whatever happened or was judged in that instance. This meant that it would be possible for the protagonist not to be in the state of perceiving in that instance, as reflected by the fact that it is possible that the protagonist could make no direct judgements in that instance. Perceiving, or the ability to make a certain kind of judgement, that is, is a separate state of the protagonist which can be seen to apply or not to apply on a certain occasion. Since it must be the case that sufficient material is provided by the laws and judgement of other instances for a true judgement to be made about the world on that occasion irrespective of what happens on it (if the world is to be a comprehensible one) then it must be possible for the protagonist to make such true judgements (for objects to exist) whatever state he is in on that occasion (whether he is perceiving or not, or whether he is able to make a certain kind of judgement or not).

This was the essence of the argument to the conclusion that it must be possible for some of the objects of the protagonist's judgements to exist unperceived. It has no direct reference to any spatial relation between the protagonist and those

objects, nor does it seem to imply such a relation. For it seems
that the argument would work just as well even if it was
specified that there was not such a relation. It seems, that is,
that the same argument could be made in respect of a particular model world in which it was laid down that there was
no question of any spatial relation holding between the protagonist and the objects of his judgements, for example the
kind of particular model worlds that were used to represent
worlds of sensations with the additional possibility of their
objects existing unperceived. In such a particular model
world, for example one composed of total states of the world
succeeding each other in a regular manner, it seems that there
is no essential reference to spatial connection between the
protagonist and his objects. Yet it seems that the above argument could be applied to them and so it could be discovered
that it must be possible for the objects of the judgements, the
states of the world, to exist unperceived.

It seems, that is, that it is possible to satisfy this requirement and to think of objects or states of the world as existing
unperceived without asking where such states are, or what
spatial relation they bear to where the protagonist is. It does
not seem necessary for this possibility to be satisfied, that is,
to ask where the protagonist is at all. It seems that he could
just be said to be experiencing a world which forms the
objects of his judgements and that there is no question of a
spatial relation holding between him and his world, of him
being at a certain position in that world, any more than there
could be any question of such a relation holding if he were
experiencing a world just of sensations. Sometimes he does
not experience or perceive the object that he can tell on other
grounds (by using the laws and other judgements) must be
there. In such a case, however, it can just be said that he does
not experience the object that he would normally be expected
to experience. It does not need to be decided where that
object is.

It might be thought, however, that this was not so, and
that if it is claimed that an object is there which is not perceived, then it must be said what could be done, or what
would have to be the case, if it is to be perceived. It might be
thought, that is, that it must be possible to show in some other
way what is special about the cases in which an object is not

perceived. It might then be claimed that this could only be done if the protagonist was in spatial relation with those objects, since cases of failure of perception could only be explained by the protagonist being at a certain position and the object being at another position. For example, it might be suggested, cases of failure of perception might be cases in which there was too great a distance between the protagonist and the object being judged, or in which judgement of some nearer object interfered with judgement of the object in question.

It needs little reflection, however, to see that this argument breaks down. It is not necessary to have another way of explaining cases of failure in perception since everything that is necessary to establish that such a failure has occurred is provided by the original argument. In the original argument it was shown that it must be possible for indirect judgements to hold that there was a certain object when no such object could be judged directly. If this occurs, it may or may not be possible to give an explanation of why it has occurred in that particular case; it is not necessary, however, that any kind of explanation should be given in order to establish that such breakdown has occurred.

It is not the case, therefore, that the feature demonstrated in §35, the feature that it must be possible for objects to exist unperceived, leads directly to the feature that there must be a spatial relation between the protagonist and at least some of the objects of his world. If this feature is to be demonstrated, therefore, it must be argued for independently, either by a new use of the features already demonstrated or else with the help of some new assumption.

§44   ACTIVE TESTING

The most promising feature from which to derive the feature that there must be a spatial relation between the protagonist and the objects of his world is the feature that it must be possible for the objects of his world to exist unperceived by him. Yet it has just been seen in the last section that such an argument can not be made. It is extremely unlikely that this desired new feature can be derived from any of the features about mistake; and it has been seen that the features which require some way of separating qualitatively identical instances can be satisfied by time alone or by another form of space. This means that it is most unlikely that this new feature can be derived with the general model world in its present condition. If it is to be derived some help will have to be given with the assumption of a new premiss and the introduction of a new feature.

It will be remembered that when time could not be derived in the state of the general model world developed from the first premiss, a new premiss was used to introduce it. The use of this second premiss moved the general model world to its second level of austerity or necessity. On this second level both the features established on the first level and the new feature introduced by the second premiss have together been used to yield the results of the last two chapters. It now appears, however, that a new premiss is needed for further argument. This new premiss will introduce a new feature which will help the argument to get started again. Its use means that the general model world will again move to a lesser level of austerity or necessity.

When new premisses are introduced to enable new starts to be made in argument, and causing breaks in the level of necessity of the general model world, such premisses are not chosen at random but are supported by inclining arguments, arguments which make their introduction natural even if they do not absolutely necessitate such an introduction. It was seen, for example, in §§27 and 28 that although an atemporal world narrowly satisfied the requirements of the first premiss, these requirements were satisfied much better in a temporal world. For in a temporal world, what was called passive testing was possible; the protagonist could make use of the judgement of new instances to test his judgement of the laws and so his judgement of previous instances. Every judgement in a temporal world, that is, is open to further test and so to further support. This obviously satisfies the first premiss in a fuller and more satisfactory way than when this is not the case. In both cases reasons are available to the protagonist, enabling him to distinguish between those of his judgements which are true and those of his judgements which are false. In the case of a temporal world, however, these reasons are better and more independent ones. This is why the premiss is more fully satisfied in a temporal world; which forms an inclining argument for the introduction of time into the general model world, although not a necessitating one.

In an analogous way to the argument of §§27 and 28, now that another break in the level of necessity of the general model world has been found to be required, such a break can be effected by a feature introduced on the basis of an inclining argument which shows that, although the first premiss can be satisfied at the present level of the world, it can be satisfied in a fuller and more complete way if this new feature is introduced. In §§27 and 28, the feature introduced was time, which was closely linked with the possibility of passive testing. The feature that will now be introduced is the possibility of active testing. Although, that is, the first premiss is obviously satisfied in a world in which the protagonist can use the new judgements he happens to make as a check upon, and as a support for, his judgements of the laws, it is obviously better satisfied if the protagonist is allowed to test those laws if he desires to do so. For if the protagonist is allowed actively to test the laws in this way, then he will obviously be able to provide more support for any judgements that he may feel doubt about, and in general will be more able to distinguish between his false and his true judgements. This forms an inclining argument for the introduction of the feature that the protagonist is able to test his judgements of the laws of his world whenever he wishes. This feature, which may be called the possibility of active testing, will be assumed in what follows, and its introduction by a new premiss marks a shift to the third level of the general model world.

Quite apart from the inclining arguments that can be produced for it, the possibility of interfering with the world and of testing the judgements that one makes about the world is obviously a central feature of our present experience of, and judgement about, our own present world. So it is interesting to see what the consequences and preconditions of such a central feature are; interesting to see what must be added to the conditions of a world being a comprehensible one in order to make it a world on which one is also able to act. The assumption of this feature, therefore, has its own independent interest quite apart from the fact that inclining arguments can be produced for it, based on the first premiss, and quite apart from the fact that it seems a convenient feature with which to make the move to the third level of austerity of the general model world.

§45   CONSEQUENCES OF ACTION UPON THE WORLD

It has now to be seen what is required in any world which is to contain the features that have already been seen to be essential in any comprehensible world and which also contains this new premised feature that the protagonist can actively test any law that he wishes to. If the protagonist tests a law he can only do so by production of an instance of that law, and then seeing whether the particular state of the world he has produced is associated with the other states of the world that the law declares it to be associated with. If, for example, one of the laws of a particular model world is 'whenever p, then q, and then r', then its protagonist could test this law at any time he wishes by producing an example of state p. He could then observe if this example of state p was followed by states q and r. If it was, this would confirm the law, if not, not.

If this way of fulfilling the new feature is looked at in more detail, however, it seems impossible that both it and the features already derived could be satisfied in one world. For suppose that this particular model world being described was such that at the time that the protagonist wished to test the law 'whenever p, then q, and then r', he was confronted by the series $x, y, z, x, y, z \ldots$ Now, if all his judgements are correct and he judges everything that he is confronted with, then he will judge, say, '$x, y, z, x, p, q, r \ldots$' Suppose that the protagonist considers such a series, for example because he wants to remember what he has experienced. He will then use the laws of his world in the same way as described in previous chapters to isolate either the second 'x' judgement or the 'p' judgement as false. A case where active testing occurs, that is, will be a case in which there is a breakdown in the normal series that are experienced or judged. This means that either such active testing cannot be allowed, and the laws used in their old way to distinguish between true and false judgements: or else that such testing is allowed, in which case it seems impossible to continue using the laws to distinguish between true and false judgements, for once active testing is allowed every case of breakdown could be a case of active testing and not a case of false judgement. It seems, that is, impossible to have both these features in a world, for satisfying one precludes satisfying the other.

It has now been assumed, however, that any comprehensible world must contain these two features, and so some way must be found by which they can both be satisfied in one world. It might be thought that this could be done in a particular model world by adding to the original laws of that world another set of laws laying down when such testing should take place. Such a law, for example, might be 'whenever the protagonist is experiencing the series x, y, z, he always tests the law about p, q, and r at the second appearance of x'. This law would indeed enable the protagonist who judged the series given above, 'x, y, z, x, p, q, r', to regard it as a true series of judgements (as describing correctly, for example, what he experienced at that time). It only enables him to do this, however, because the introduction of such laws would eliminate the other feature, the feature of active testing, from any world in which they held. For the point of active testing is that the protagonist can test (at least some of) the laws of his world whenever he desires to. If, however, a world contains such laws about when he tests, then he can never test any laws when he desires to but, instead, must wait for the occasion specified in such laws before any testing takes place. When such an occasion arrives, the protagonist must test in the way that the law lays down. He never, that is, possesses any option about whether to test or not, or about what to test. So this is again an example of a case in which the introduction of one feature inhibits the introduction of the other; contrary to first appearances, this world does not contain the feature of active testing.

The idea behind the proposal to introduce laws about when testing takes place was a sound one, even if the proposal itself was unsuccessful. This idea is that all the phenomena of a comprehensible world must be covered by laws which link judgement about any part of these phenomena to judgement about other parts of these phenomena. There cannot be total gaps between judgements about one part of it and judgements about other parts, otherwise it would be impossible to decide whether such judgements were true or false. The phenomena, that is, must be law-covered, and it is just this, at least at first sight, which is impossible in a world in which active testing is allowed. The answer to the problem must be to find a way in which all (or most) of the phenomena can still remain law-covered and yet in which options can still be left open to the protagonist about what he is going to experience or confront himself with. This means that a solution will not be found to this problem as long as the only laws being considered are laws which satisfy the general format 'whenever α, then β'; laws, that is, which lay down definitely and absolutely what must follow something else. For such laws leave no option open to the protagonist, and mean that anything which is open to his option is not law-covered.

There can be laws, however, other than those which satisfy the format 'whenever α, then β'. For example, there can be laws which lay down two alternatives which may follow upon something; which specify that one of the alternatives must follow but do not specify which. Such laws satisfy the general format 'whenever α, then either β or γ'. It is obvious that on these lines a solution can be found to the problem of this section. For with such laws, the whole phenomena of a world could be law-covered and yet options would be left open to the protagonist. In a world containing such laws, that is, laws would be available to the protagonist which enabled him to distinguish between his true judgements and his false judgements. Yet in a world in which all the phenomena were totally covered by such laws, choice would still be left open to the protagonist about what he confronted or experienced, and so in such a world active testing of the laws would be possible.

It will be remembered that when the consequences of the first premiss were being derived in §18, it was discovered not only that there must be laws in any comprehensible world which enable judgement of one instance to be connected up with judgement of another instance, but that the judgement of one particular instance must be connected up with the judgement of many other instances, so that the judgement of all these other instances could be used to provide pressure on this single instance, pressure which was sufficient to support it as true or sufficient to isolate it as false. This connecting up of one instance with many other instances was achieved in the particular model worlds that were created in that section since these particular model worlds consisted of states following each other in a continuous cycle; this meant that a few simple laws which specified the cycle enabled any one judgement to be connected up with as many other judgements as desired, and if necessary the pressure of thousands of judgements could be applied to any one judgement.

This requirement can also be satisfied in a world whose laws are the kind of alternative laws represented by the format 'whenever α, then β or γ '. For the two possible states mentioned as successors at the end of such laws may themselves have laws about them stating the various alternatives that can follow them. In this way two states of the model world that are linked together by one such law may themselves each be linked with other states by other such laws, and these states with yet other states. It is possible, that is, to have a set of such laws expressing alternatives so that judgements about many different instances are connected together, and the pressure of judgements about many instances applied to the judgement of one instance in order to see whether that judgement is true or false.

An example of such linking of the states of a particular model world with each other by means of a set of alternative laws would be provided if the laws could be expressed, for example, by the following schema:

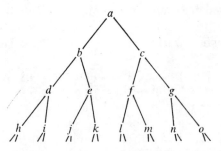

The protagonist here is supposed to be able to confront himself with the series of objects described by any vertical route through the schema. Thus, after confronting an a, the protagonist may confront himself either with a b or a c, on confronting himself with a c, he may confront himself either with an f or a g, and so on. This schema is therefore shorthand for a set of alternative laws, the individual members of the set being laws like 'whenever a, then either b or c', 'whenever c, then either f or g', and so on. It is obvious that all the objects in this world are connected together by means of laws, so that one true judgement can be supported by many other judgements, and a false judgement isolated by its non-agreement with many other judgements. If, for example, the protagonist of this world judged 'a, c, g, n . . .', then these judgements would all support each other. On the other hand, if he judged 'a, c, e, n . . .', then the laws could be used to isolate the judgement 'e' as false. So in this particular model world, the laws could be used to provide support for some judgements, and to isolate other judgements as false just as they could in some of the particular model worlds being discussed above where only laws of the kind 'whenever a, then β', were being considered. In both cases it is possible for the laws to meet the requirement that the pressure of many cases can be applied to the judgement of one single instance, and so in both cases can the laws be used (with other such judgements) to distinguish between those judgements which are true and those judgements which are false.

This particular model world can, therefore, meet certain of the requirements that were seen before to be essential in any comprehensible world. It can, however, also contain the new feature that has been introduced in the present chapter, the possibility of active testing. For suppose that the protagonist is confronted with an a and wants to test the alternative law of the world 'whenever c, then f or g'. In order to do this he chooses to confront himself with c (rather than b), and then observes that f (or g) follows. If he judges that they do, this will provide support for the law, if not, not. Here the protagonist does not need merely to wait and see what happens, as in the abortive proposal that there could be laws which laid down when he made tests. Instead he can himself choose to test a law that he is interested in. If, for example, he had been interested in testing the law 'whenever b, then d or e' while he was at a, then he would have chosen to confront himself with b rather than with c. So this model world also contains the feature that active testing is possible, and shows how alternative laws (laws expressing alternatives) can be used to combine the feature that all the objects of the world must be connected together in a law-like manner with the feature that it must be possible to test those laws when it is desired to do so.

Of course it may be the case in this particular model world that some laws cannot be tested directly. If, for example, the protagonist wants to test the law 'whenever f, then l or m' while he is at a, then he will not be able to confront himself directly with f. He will have first to confront himself with c and then confront himself with f. However, this still leaves the position different from the position described in the suggestion that there should be laws stating when tests are made. For even though the protagonist has to confront himself with certain states of the world in order to confront himself with certain other states, this does not mean that he is not able to choose the states with which he is to be confronted. It only lays down how he has to carry out such choices. It lays down, that is, in more detail what he has to do in order to confront himself with the kind of state that he wants to confront himself with. This does not mean that he is not able to confront himself with any kind of state that he desires to, and so able to test any law he wishes. The feature of active testing, therefore, is contained in this particular model world together with at least some of the other features that have been seen to be essential in any comprehensible world.

§46 VOLITIONS

The device of using laws expressing alternatives, therefore, is one way in which the feature introduced in this chapter can be contained in the same worlds that contain the features that have earlier been shown to be essential in any comprehensible world. This, however, does not mean that laws expressing alternatives have been shown to be an essential feature of the general model world at its present level. For to show this it would have not only to be shown that laws expressing alternatives was a way of combining the new feature with the original ones, but it would also have to be shown that there was no other way of making such a combination. In this section this will be attempted by showing that the only apparent alternative to the use of laws expressing alternatives is not in fact a tenable one.

This apparent alternative is to presume that the protagonist possesses states of mind which can be called volitions.

It might be suggested, that is, that whenever the protagonist of a certain particular model world wishes to test the laws of that world, he is at that time in a certain state which can be described as possessing a volition to test that law. The laws of this particular model world might, for example, be the same as the laws of particular model worlds described in earlier chapters, so that the model world consisted of states which succeeded each other in a regular cyclic fashion. Sometimes, however, the protagonist of it, instead of awaiting events, might want to test one of his laws. When he wants to do this he confronts himself immediately with a relevant instance, and so tests the law.

It was objected in the last section that the protagonist could not do this without making it the case that the world no longer possessed the feature that its objects were connected together by laws. In particular, it seemed that if a protagonist could do this it would not be possible to distinguish the apparently strange combination of judgements that were due to the protagonist wanting to test a law in this manner and the apparently strange combinations of judgements that were due to the protagonist making mistake in judgement. The point of the present suggestion, however, is to provide a means of making such a distinction. For an apparently strange combination of judgements due to active testing would be distinguished from such a combination due to mistake by the presence of a volition in the former case. Similarly, although all the objects of the world would not be connected together in a law-like manner, it would be easy to tell when such laws applied and when they did not. For whenever a volition was present, then the laws would not apply but whenever there was no volition then the laws would apply and could be relied on.

This suggestion obviously allows the possibility of active testing. For in the particular model world just described it is possible for the protagonist to test any law he wants at any time. He merely has the appropriate volition and confronts himself with the relevant instance while he refrains from further volitions in order to see what follows upon that instance. The only question remaining to be decided, therefore, is whether this particular model world has its objects connected together in the law-like way that is necessary for the first premiss to be satisfied. The question is, that is, whether the presence of a volition is sufficient to enable the protagonist to distinguish between breakdowns caused by active testing and breakdowns caused by mistake, or whether something else necessary in any comprehensible world would be omitted in a world in which volitions were used in this way.

Suppose a case is taken in which this protagonist is concerned to isolate a judgement as false, for example is concerned to detect a memory as merely being an apparent memory rather than a real one. If there were no active testing or volitions, the protagonist would do this by seeing whether the sequence of objects that he seemed to remember judging fell under the laws of that particular world or not. If, for example, the laws were 'always b after a', then the protagonist could distinguish an apparent memory which went 'a, b' as true and an apparent memory which went 'a, p' as false. If active testing is possible, and if the protagonist can always confront himself with any object at will, then this is no longer a possible way of distinguishing between genuine and merely apparent memories. For it could be the case that the protagonist actually had experienced a, p, for it could be the case that after having been confronted with a he decided to test some law about p. One solution for this was proposed in the last section, where it was proposed that the laws could be about alternatives. Another solution is proposed in the present section and is that the case in which the judgement 'a, p' expresses a false memory can be distinguished from the case in which it expresses a true one because in the latter case it is accompanied by another memory, the memory of the volition to test that law. It is suggested, that is, that in a case of active testing something else is around, namely a volition. So if this case is being remembered something different will be remembered, since as well as the objects judged, the volition will also be remembered. If, for example, 'V' stands for volition, then in the case of false memory 'a, p' will be judged whereas in the case of true memory 'a, V, p' will be judged; the volition distinguishes them.

If some of the conditions of a world being a comprehensible one which were repeated in the last section are remembered, it will be seen that this way of making the distinction between true and false judgements (for example, between real and apparent memories) is not good enough. For, as was emphasized there, it is essential in any comprehensible world that the pressure of many judgements can be applied to any particular judgement in order to determine whether it is true or false. This was why it was essential to show that a set of laws expressing alternatives could be linked together by the kind of schema that was given at the end of the last section. Yet this is just what cannot happen in the present case. For the only judgement (or memory) that can be produced to show that there was a volition causing the apparent break is the judgement (or memory) of the volition itself. This judgement is supported by no other judgement, and so cannot be the means of getting the pressure of many other judgements to apply on one particular judgement.

The distinction between a break which reveals mistake in judgement from a break which reveals that there has been active testing, that is, depends only on the presence or absence of one other judgement. No further independent support can be provided for this single judgement over and above the fact that it is associated with an apparent break in the normal laws, which is what provided the original problem that volitions were meant to solve, and so cannot be used to support one solution of the problem rather than another. In the kinds of model world described in previous chapters, that is, a particular judgement could be supported by another judgement, this other judgement by another and the process carried on as far as desired. Such connection of judgements, in which the pressure of many judgements could be applied to one particular judgement in order to decide whether it was true or false, was held to be essential in §18. Yet in this present suggestion the difference between a judgement being held to be true and its being held to be false is made by the presence or absence of one other judgement, is made by whether the case is 'a, V, p' or whether it is 'a, p'. Yet no other support is possible for this 'V', no other judgements that the protagonist makes or has made can help in deciding whether that volition was present or not. So in this case the essential condition is lacking, the pressure of many other judgements cannot be applied to a single case of judgement in order to decide between its being true and its being false. Volitions cannot therefore be used as a way of providing active testing in a world which satisfies the features that have already been discovered to be essential. This can be taken as a demonstration that the only way that there can be active testing in a world which meets these conditions is if at least some of the laws of that world are laws which express alternatives. So a feature that follows from the new feature of the possibility of active testing is that there must be laws expressing alternatives in the world.

§47 FURTHER CONSEQUENCES OF ACTION

It has now been demonstrated that the general world at this level contains the feature that some at least of the laws are laws expressing alternatives rather than direct consequences. It was seen in §45 that such laws must form a set so that many different judgements can be connected together. Such a set was embodied in the schema given at the end of §45, which will be repeated here for convenience:

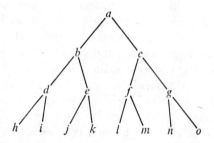

The laws embodied in such a schema enable the pressure of many judgements to be brought to bear on one particular judgement to determine whether it is true or false. For example, if the protagonist judged 'a, c, e, m', then the judgements 'a', 'c', 'm' could together be brought to bear on the judgement 'e', and so could isolate it as false.

It is obvious that volitions could be added to a model world described by this schema. The protagonist might, for example, be thought of as having two different volitions, V_1 and V_2. When he has V_1 he is confronted by the alternative on the left of the above schema, when he has V_2 he is confronted with the alternative on the right. For example, at a V_1 produces b and V_2 produces c. In such a model world volitions could be used to help in distinguishing between true and false judgements. For example, the protagonist will be able to distinguish the chain 'a, V_2, c, V_1, f . . .' as embodying true judgements or memories. This is because, since there are alternative laws, these volitions may themselves be supported and can themselves form part of a chain which applies the pressure of many judgements to one particular judgement. Remembering 'a, V_2, c', that is, is exactly what would be expected and so all these judgements support each other. Although volitions by themselves, therefore, are not sufficient to combine the feature of active testing with the features demonstrated earlier, there is no reason why they cannot be used in a world containing laws which express alternatives.

In §18, however, it was not only shown that the laws must be such that the judgement of several instances can be connected together. It was also shown that the laws themselves must be relatively simple in nature or number so that they could be applied by the protagonist to many cases, both old and new ones, both ones he was certain of and ones he wanted to examine. This is why the particular model worlds described in previous chapters had one simple set of laws, for example expressing the cyclical order that the states of that world went through, which could be applied to infinitely many instances. This meant both that it was always easy to tell which law was the relevant one and also that all laws were continually open to check or refutation (for they were continually being applied to a new lot of instances).

This essential feature is obviously lacking in the model world whose laws are expressed in the schema repeated at the beginning of this chapter. For in that schema each law is only operated once. The schema, that is, shows how the protagonist may judge correctly after judging 'a', but it does not show how the protagonist could judge 'a' more than once (correctly). Each instance, that is, needs a separate law to cover it and there are as many instances as there are laws. This means that it is impossible to check laws that have been used and that an indefinitely large number of laws are needed. The schema is obviously expanding the whole time, and so the more of it that is given, the more complex it will be and the less likely that any particular bit of it will actually be used. This particular world, therefore, does not satisfy features which have been found to be essential in any comprehensible world. In it laws can indeed be tested, but not any laws which have already been used, and so not any laws in which there might be interest. The laws which have been used, which are exactly the laws that the protagonist will want to be able to check if he is checking up on the accuracy of his memories, are just the laws that he is unable to check. The laws he is able to check are not ones he has ever used, and so ones in which he can have little interest.

More than just a set of alternative laws is needed, therefore, if both the new feature introduced in the present chapter, and also the features already derived, are to be contained in a single model world. Such laws will also have to be arranged so that it is possible for the protagonist to test laws which cover the instances he has judged in the past. The laws, that is, will have to be such that the same laws cover several occasions; will have to be such that after a certain time all or nearly all of the instances judged are covered by laws already known and previously used. For this to happen there must obviously be some repetition in the states of the world with which the protagonist is confronted, just as there was repetition in the states of the simpler model worlds constructed in previous chapters.

Such repetition could be created in a model world in several ways. It could be created, for example, by combining laws about alternatives with laws laying down unique successors so that, whatever the protagonist had to choose to confront himself with at certain times, he had inevitably to be confronted with certain states at other times. The laws of such a model world could be expressed, for example, in the schema shown opposite.

This schema obviously starts in the same way as the one above, but then tapers in to the original state so that repetitions can take place. In the model world whose laws are represented by this schema, if the protagonist is confronted with an *a*, a *b* or a *c*, then he has a choice about the next feature with which he is to be confronted. At any other time, however, he has to be entirely passive. An *e*, for example, cannot but be followed by an *h*, nor an *h* by anything but an *a*.

In this model world its protagonist obviously has some control over which laws shall be tested. Suppose, for example, he wishes to test the law 'whenever *f*, then *i*' while he is confronted with an *h*. He cannot but wait for *a* to succeed *h*, for he can have no choice whenever he is confronted with an *h*. Once he is confronted with *a*, however, then he can choose to confront himself with *c*, and then choose to confront himself with *f* and so test the law. So some of the choice that was contained in the previous schema is retained by this one, and

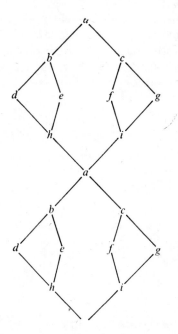

this one can satisfy the features required in any comprehensible world in a way that the previous one cannot. For the laws represented by this schema are such that each law is used several times, such that a few laws cover all the instances, and so the laws of interest to the protagonist can both be known to him and tested by him.

On the other hand, in this particular model world the possibility of control over what state the world is in, or judged directly to be in, only exists for half of the time. So for half of the time the possibility embraced in the new feature, the possibility of active testing, is satisfied. For the other half, the protagonist has no choice over what he is being confronted with, and there is no difference between his situation at such times and his situation in a world in which there is no possibility of active testing. It is at least interesting, therefore, and may turn out to be vital later, to see what kind of model world would both contain repetitions, and so have a few laws covering all the instances, and yet be one in which the protagonist always had a choice about which feature he was to be confronted with next.

It seems that such a model world would have to be one in which the schema representing the laws kept expanding, and so kept offering alternatives, and yet one in which the same states kept reappearing. Such a model world would be described, for example, by the following schema:

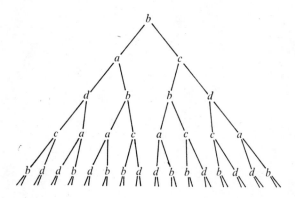

Such a schema may appear at first sight to be very complex, but on further examination it can be seen to be composed of a few simple laws constantly repeated. The same state is always followed in the same way by the same choice of states with which that state is to be succeeded. If the protagonist is allowed to make two operations on the world, corresponding to the two volitions mentioned at the beginning of this section, so that O_1 always produces the state shown on the left of the two alternatives mentioned in the schema and O_2 always produces the state shown on the right, then, for example, state b with operation O_1 always produces state a, state a with O_1 always produces state d and so on. This schema is therefore not as complex as it looks and simply represents the following set of laws:

$$b + O_1 = a$$
$$b + O_2 = c$$
$$a + O_1 = d$$
$$a + O_2 = b$$
$$c + O_1 = b$$
$$c + O_2 = d$$
$$d + O_1 = c$$
$$d + O_2 = a$$

These laws produce the schema as it is given, extended as far as is desired. So all the instances are covered by comparatively few laws. These laws are the same as covered past instances and so are ones which a protagonist may be interested in testing. At the same time they are laws which will cover future instances, and so may be tested. A particular model world which contains these laws, therefore, will be one which satisfies the features which were seen earlier to be required by any comprehensible world. At the same time this particular model world is one in which the protagonist has at every time a choice about which feature he is to be confronted with next. So at any time he can operate upon the world in a way that is relevant to his desire to test a particular law. It is a world, therefore, in which the possibility of active testing is always present.

In case this particular model world still looks complex, it should be pointed out that the way that states are connected together in it is really extremely simple. This was disguised by the schema laying down the choices at any time, and may still be partly concealed by the complete set of laws that has just been given. Its simplicity is revealed, however, if another way of representing the laws is adopted in which all the possible kinds of states are written down and then all the states a protagonist may confront himself with after a particular state represented by arrows. If an exercise of operation one is represented by a dotted arrow and an exercise of operation two is represented by a continuous arrow, then this particular model world can have all its laws represented by the simple diagram shown overleaf.

This makes it quite clear how simple the laws are, and so

how the relevant laws cover any number of instances. It also shows how the laws can be used to provide support for true judgements and to isolate false ones. For example, the following series of judgements could be distinguished as true: '*a, d, c, d, c, b* . . .'; whereas in the following series the judgement '*b*' could be isolated as false: '*a, d, a, d, b* . . .'

In this section further features that were seen in §18 to be required in any comprehensible world have been reconsidered, and particular model worlds have been examined to see how such features could be combined in a single model world with the new feature introduced in the present chapter, the possibility of active testing. It was decided that the

schema given in §45 would not satisfy these further requirements. So it has been seen that a particular model world which is to represent the general model world at this level must either be such that active testing is only possible part of the time or else be the kind of world represented by sets of interconnected laws similar to the set just given, sets which can be expressed in diagrams such as the diagram just above.

§48 SPACE

It has now been seen that a feature of the general model world at this level (and so of any comprehensible world as specified by the first three premisses) is that it must contain a set of laws expressing alternatives so that judgements about one instance must be connected up with judgements about many other instances. It has been seen that there must be relatively few such laws so that the same laws can be used and tested on several separate occasions. This has been seen to involve some repetition in the instances covered by the laws, and some ways in which this could be achieved have been described in the last section. In a world with active testing, the laws that a protagonist will wish to test are those that apply to instances that have already been judged. They will, therefore, be laws about the kind of states with which the protagonist has already been acquainted. To test such laws the protagonist must re-confront himself with such states. Testing, therefore, will involve the repetition of states, and so of the laws covering the connection of those states. The protagonist must be able at will to confront himself with states of the same kind as the states he has previously encountered.

The laws expressing alternatives in a particular model world will lay down the particular states that a protagonist must confront himself with in order to be confronted with any desired state. They will lay down the intermediary states that a protagonist must confront himself with when he is confronted with any one particular state and wishes to confront himself with any other particular state. So, for example, in the particular model world described at the end of the last section, a protagonist who is confronted with an a, and wishes to confront himself with a c, must confront himself with a b. In the particular model world described before that, in which the protagonist was able to choose only half of the time which state he should be confronted with, if he was confronted with an a and wished to be confronted with an h, for example, then the laws lay down that he must confront himself with a b and then with an e. The laws of these model worlds, that is, lay down the intermediaries which must be confronted in order to confront any particular (kind of) state.

The set of laws expressing alternatives that is required, therefore, is a set which lays down the intermediary states which must be confronted between confrontation with any particular (kind of) state and confrontation with any other particular (kind of) state. It is essential to have such intermediaries otherwise no use could be made of laws in distinguishing between true and false judgements. If, as was seen above, the protagonist could immediately confront himself with any state he wished, then it would be impossible to say which series of judgements contained true judgements and which false. If, however, there are intermediary states which must be confronted between confrontation with any two particular states, then judgement of such intermediaries will

show that a series of judgements is true, and lack of judgement of such intermediaries will show that a series of judgements is false (or that it contains false members). On the
other hand it is essential that the laws producing such intermediaries should be a set which lays down exactly which
intermediaries should be confronted in order to be confronted
with any desired state. For the point of the laws expressing
alternatives is that they should enable the protagonist to test
any laws he wishes. He will not be able to do this unless he
can confront himself with any state that he wishes to confront
himself with, and he will not be able to do this unless the
laws specify all the intermediate states that he needs to confront himself with while he is confronted with any particular
state in order to be confronted with any other particular
state.

These laws which lay down such complete sets of intermediaries which must be confronted between confrontation
with any two particular states can be taken to express a dimension. For they order states in such a way that they show exactly
which states must be traversed in order to arrive at any particular state. This is particularly clear in the particular model
world which gave fullest expression to the feature that active
testing should be possible, the particular model world which
was described at the end of the last section and whose laws
could be expressed succinctly by means of the following
diagram:

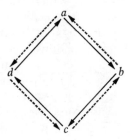

Here the diagram shows that in order to confront c, for
example, while confronting a, a protagonist must either confront d or b. It is possible to represent the laws in such a
simple diagram just because it is possible to take the laws as
representing a dimension, in this case space. The laws of this

particular model world, that is, express exactly how the world would be if it consisted of four states arranged in a ring with the protagonist being allowed to travel around the ring in either direction.

This becomes clearer still when it is remembered that the two different kinds of arrow express the two different operations that the protagonist can make upon his world in order to confront himself with a desired state. The dotted arrow represents operation one and the continuous arrow operation two. Once it is seen that the laws of this particular model world express the way that its states are connected together with each other in space, it is easy to see what these two operations are. Operation one, the one expressed by the dotted arrow, will be moving around the ring in one direction, say anti-clockwise, while operation two, the one expressed by the continuous arrow, will be moving around the ring in the other direction. Once this particular model world is taken to consist of states spatially connected together in this way, it is easy to see why the laws expressing alternatives lay down the intermediaries which must be traversed between any two particular states. For not every state is adjacent to every other; the states are ordered in space. On the other hand it can be seen that the protagonist can confront himself with any state he desires; for by using the appropriate operations (by moving in the appropriate direction) through the appropriate intermediaries (the appropriate distance), the protagonist can change his relation with the world so that he can move from confrontation with any one particular state to any other particular state.

A set of laws that satisfies the requirements of a comprehensible world, therefore, will be a complete set linking any state with any other state and will express exactly the intermediaries that must be traversed between confrontation with any one state and confrontation with any other state. Such a set, therefore, will order all the states of the world. It must also express alternative means of traversing this order, since it must be possible for the protagonist to choose to confront himself with any state he wishes to. The order the states must be in in order to satisfy such laws is the kind of order imposed by a dimension. Yet it is an additional ordering to that imposed by time and so must be imposed by another dimension to time. This can be seen from the fact that it must be possible to have choice about how the order is to be traversed, whereas it is not usually thought to be possible that there should be choice about the direction in which time should be traversed.

The alternative laws that are seen to be required, therefore, express a dimension and it is another dimension to time. They express, that is, choices about which states should be confronted with as time progresses. The states chosen are ordered in a dimension so that certain states must be traversed in order to get to certain other states. This dimension, not being time, must be space. This was clearly seen in the particular example of the particular model world described at the end of the last section. Here the set of laws was seen to express how the states of that world were connected together in space; and it was because these states were connected together in space that the laws of the model world could be represented by the simple diagram that was given at the end of that section.

Once the feature of the possibility of active testing, therefore, is added to the features already derived another feature that any comprehensible world must possess is that its states are ordered in another dimension to time, a dimension through which the protagonist can move as he pleases. This seems to be a sufficient demonstration of the necessity of space in any comprehensible world (as specified by the first three premises). In any case, it certainly shows the central place that space has in our own system and how it is space that enables us to act as we wish upon the world in our own present case.

In §42 it was remarked that it was not just space as such that was to be examined in this section but that there should be spatial relations between the protagonist and the objects of his world. This more specific feature is the one which is demonstrated by the above argument. For the set of alternative laws that is seen to be required in any particular model world which is to satisfy the three premises lays down how the protagonist must move in order to get from any one particular state to any other particular state. The alternative laws that are required, that is, do not only mean that the states of the world are in spatial relation with each other but that they are also in spatial relation with the protagonist. For they depend for their operation on the protagonist being at one position in his world, depend upon him being confronted by one feature. It is because he is at a certain position in the world that the laws can lay down how he can get to any other position that he chooses to get to. So the feature demonstrated in this chapter is not just space as such but the more specific feature that the protagonist must be in spatial relation with the objects of his world.

§49 EXISTENCE UNPERCEIVED

It follows from the argument of the last section that the general model world at this level must also contain the feature that it must be possible for the objects of a world to exist unperceived by its protagonist. This feature was demonstrated at the previous level of the general model world in §35. The argument there, however, was somewhat tortuous and it is interesting to realize that this feature can be derived more simply at the present level of the model world.

The feature that it must be possible for objects to exist unperceived follows from the previous section because it has been shown in that section that spatial relations must exist between the state of the world that is confronted with, and so perceived, at any one time and other states of that world. If these states are in spatial relation with each other, then they must all exist simultaneously. Only one of them, however, is perceived. This means that the other states must exist at that time unperceived. The laws expressing alternatives, that is, lay down which states must be traversed so that some particular state is confronted with and perceived; this particular state at present exists without being so confronted with or perceived, and the laws lay down how it can be perceived.

It follows, therefore, from the particular way in which such laws have been demonstrated that it must be possible for the states of a model world to exist unperceived. It will be noticed that it does not follow just from the particular feature demonstrated in the last section, for it would be perfectly possible for the protagonist to be in spatial relation with the objects of his world without there being any question of those objects being able to exist unperceived. He could, that is, perceive everything that there was in his world and still have a spatial position in it, so that he was closer to certain objects in it than to others, even though he always perceived both lots of objects. The possibility of objects existing unperceived, therefore, does not just follow from the feature demonstrated in the last section. It depends also upon the particular way that it was demonstrated there.

It depends in particular upon the feature that active testing is possible. For if active testing is to be possible in a world, the protagonist must be able to confront himself with a state or object that he is at that moment not confronted with. There must, that is, be states other than the states that the protagonist is confronted with, or perceives, at any one time. This does not by itself mean that such states need exist when they are not confronted with, or perceived. It merely means that it must be possible for the protagonist to confront himself with other states than the state he is confronted with at any one time, whether or not these other states exist before he is confronted with them.

In the last section, however, it was shown that these other states that the protagonist could confront if he wished have spatial relations with the state that he is at present confronting. This means that they must exist at the same time as this state, and so means that they must exist unperceived. So it follows from the particular way in which the argument for spatial connection must be made rather than the conclusion at which it arrives that it must be possible for the states or objects of a comprehensible world to exist unperceived. For only if this is possible can the kind of spatial relation seen to be required in the last section be combined with the possibility of active testing assumed at the beginning of this chapter.

It is a feature of the general model world at this level, then, that the states of it perceived by the protagonist at any one time are connected to the states not perceived by him by a spatial relation, so that it is possible for the protagonist to move from these former states to the latter, and so perceive them. These states, both those which are perceived at that time and those that are not, exist simultaneously in that such spatial relations exist between them. So the states that are not perceived exist unperceived; the feature developed and demonstrated with great difficulty in Chapter Five follows directly from the arguments and conclusions of the present chapter.

§50   THE GENERAL MODEL WORLD

This has been an inquiry into the essential features of any comprehensible world. In order to start the argument off, and in order to renew it when it has got stuck, various features have been assumed to be features of any comprehensible world. The preconditions of these assumptions have then been examined, and the preconditions of those preconditions, in order to see what other features are required by these assumptions, and so to see what other features are essential in any comprehensible world. In the inquiry there were three such assumptions introduced at the appropriate time by three premisses. The picture of the features essential in any comprehensible world that has been built up has been thought of, and described, as the building of the general model world. This general model world has had three levels corresponding to the three premisses used in the inquiry. First something obviously essential in any comprehensible world was assumed, and it was seen what other features were required by it. This formed the first level of the general model world. When no more argument was possible, and no more features could be derived, another feature was assumed by means of the second premiss. With the use of this second assumption the general model world moved to its second level and several further features were derived. When another assumption was required the third assumption was introduced by the third premiss in exactly the same way as the previous two.

As the first premiss it was assumed that reasons must be available to the protagonist enabling him to distinguish between those judgements of his which are true and those judgements of his which are false. From this premiss there were derived the features that the world must be connected together so that the truth of some judgements could form reasons for the truth or falsity of other judgements, that this connection had to be law-like in manner, and that the protagonist had to be able to prefer a judgement based on the laws of a particular world to what he would otherwise directly judge the situation to be. These features form the inmost level of the general model world, the level at which it is most certain that its features are features of any comprehensible world whatsoever.

It was then attempted to derive time from these features. This was ultimately discovered to be impossible, even though good inclining arguments for accepting time were produced, and even though certain other features such as the necessity of either space or time were derived. Time was accordingly assumed in the second premiss and, with its assumption, the general model world moved to its second level of necessity or certainty. At this level it was shown to be the case that it must be possible for a protagonist to be in error in his direct present judgements about what he is confronted with. Derivation of this feature showed that many phenomenalist accounts are based on a false picture of the essential conditions of any world being a comprehensible one. It was seen that this feature did not imply the feature that it must be possible for objects to exist unperceived, nor did it imply the feature that it must be possible for objects to be perceived by more than one person. The private language argument was accordingly criticized and the means by which it criticized phenomenalism and attempted to establish the possibility of existence unperceived was attacked. Another feature derived at this level was this possibility of existence unperceived, which was established in a completely independent manner.

The general model world moved to its third level with the assumption that it must be possible to have action, and active testing, in any comprehensible world. From this assumption the feature has just been derived that there must be spatial relations between the protagonist and the objects of his world, and a simpler argument has just been produced for the possibility of existence unperceived.

Index